FOUNDING *Women:*

Inspiration and Impact on Chautauqua and the Nation

FOUNDING Women:
Inspiration and Impact on Chautauqua and the Nation

By Janet Myers Northrup
& The Chautauqua Women's Club
Chautauqua, New York

Mountain Air Books

Mountain Air Books
27 Portsmouth Terrace, Ste. #1
Rochester, NY 14607

Email: Mairbooks123@yahoo.com

Layout/ Design: Scott Krause
Cover: Scott Krause and Tibb Middleton
Cover photo: Tibb Middleton
Contributors: Mary K. Dougherty, Anita Ferguson, Marjorie Kemper, Joan Keogh, Jane Lahey, Mary Ann McCabe, Meredith Rousseau, Barbara Vackar.

ISBN: 978-0-615-29829-0

This book is dedicated to my parents, Gladys and Erskine Myers, who brought me to Chautauqua, to Dr. Helen Overs, who furthered the educational programs of Chautauqua Institution and SUNY Fredonia, and to Dave Northrup for his patience.

This book is dedicated also to the Chautauqua Women's Club members who serve, share and learn each summer at Chautauqua Institution. May the next century of the CWC show continued success, harmony, leadership and growth.

This photo was taken following the first official meeting of the Chautauqua Women's Club in 1889. The session was held at the Hall of Philosophy and then adjourned. Women posed in front of the Lewis Miller cottage, which is now a National Historic site at Chautauqua Institution. Unofficially, women had been meeting as the "Women's Club" of the Chautauqua Assembly since 1874.

TABLE OF CONTENTS

The Chautauqua Women's Club
ℭ Presidents ℬ

Emily Huntington Miller 1889-1895
Sarah Elizabeth Vincent 1896-1916
Anna J. H. Pennybacker 1917-1937
Jennie Stuart Wilson Alexander 1938
Josephine Schain 1938-1943
Mary Frances Bestor Cram 1944-1945
Helen Chapman 1946-1953
Lucy Milligan 1954-1958
Dorothy Houghton 1958-1963
Dr. Helen D. Bragdon 1963-1967
Dr. E. Dorothy Dann Bullock 1967-1979
Mary Frances Bestor Cram (interim) 1980
Margaret Hasebroock 1980-1982
Marian Clements 1983-1986
Meredith Rousseau 1987
Dorothy Clark (acting) 1988
Margaret Arnold (interim) 1988
Carolyn Markowski 1989-1991
Meredith Rousseau 1992-2001
Dr. Mary Monsen Kunze 2002-2004
Mary Ann McCabe (interim) 2004-2005
Barbara Ellison Vackar 2005-

℘ Directors Emeritae ℘

Toni Branch
Geneva Cherry
Dorothy Clark
Beverly Dame Esch
Jane Hawthorne
Elinor Johnson
Gwen Read

The Clubhouse set up for a meeting,
the beginning of many educational and
entertaining gatherings

INTRODUCTION

People who visit Chautauqua Institution today are enchanted with the beauty of the place, the quality of its programs and the aura of its history. The streets and landmarks echo the names of Chautauqua leaders from the past including: Massey, Pratt, Hurlbut, Bestor, Hazlett, Seaver, Miller and Vincent. Of course those founding fathers that came to Chautauqua were not alone. Many arrived at the steamship dock called "Fair Point" with their wives, mothers, sisters or daughters. Sometimes their steamer trunks were unloaded with them, but often the luggage was late. What was the daily life for those women at Chautauqua? Their names, other than a comparatively new street honoring Mina Miller Edison, do not occupy the street signs. How did the "founding women" of 1874 (wearing long dresses, layers of undergarments, bonnets, bustles and corsets) survive Chautauqua's hot days or, even worse, rainy ones? What were their complaints, causes, joys, interests, obligations and concerns? Where did they live on "the grounds" and where did they eat? Where did they shop, do laundry or wash in the days before indoor plumbing? Did the Chautauqua experience really help them in their lives after they left the Assembly? Was the Chautauqua experience actually a "vacation" for them? Some publications show what men accomplished at Chautauqua in the early days, but what successes did the women have?

When CWC President Barbara Vackar asked me if I would be interested in researching the history of the Chautauqua Women's Club, the idea was appealing because I wanted to learn more about women's experiences and stories at Chautauqua. I knew little about the Women's Club except their well-advertised Flea Market and annual Strawberry Festival, both of which most Chautauquans have attended enthusiastically. I was not a member of the CWC and wondered if that outsider status was an advantage or disadvantage in researching a history project. Obviously, some women had been a part of the Club for decades and knew who was involved in the leadership positions and activities. I asked a lot of questions, listened to many stories and was impressed with the answers. Everyone was helpful. The Women's Club building has filed scrapbooks from the 1950's through 2008 as well as notebooks with minutes from Board Meetings. All were valuable resources for information in this book. Eventually I was led to three works written about the Club's earlier years. A four-page pamphlet and a booklet, written by CWC President Dr. E. Dorothy Dann Bullock, were valuable resources, written around the time of the Clubhouse's 50th anniversary in the late 1970's. The third valuable resource was a short book about the CWC, written by Chautauqua Institution's renowned historian Alfreda Irwin. Her booklet also included information about the early CWC presidents and club history until 1989.

These three sources did not include pictures, but I realized photos could play a large part in explaining the history and influence of women at Chautauqua and especially those who were involved with the Women's Club. The pictures help to make the experiences of former Chautauqua days come alive. One example is the 1903 picture of CWC women gathering at the unfinished second Hall of Philosophy with a large tarp serving as the roof. The meeting conditions must have been uncomfortable on many days. In fact, the second (current) Hall of Philosophy was not completed until 1906, so hardships occurred for several "Seasons." Consequently, this book differs from the earlier historical accounts because current technology puts faces to the names of people who dedicated so much to the CWC.

In addition to the short books by Dr. Bullock and Mrs. Irwin, two other treasures I found were Jane Lahey and Mary Ann McCabe, active CWC members who contributed to the production of this book. They often made suggestions about where to look for information, reminded me of what was important (or not) and knew about the contributions of various members and group activities. This book would not have been written without their input, assistance and encouragement. Both helped select pictures from the scrapbooks, scanned the photos and assisted with the editing. They are knowledgeable, hard working, dedicated, fun and affable.

The Oliver Archives personnel were helpful as well. Special thanks goes to Jason Rodriguez for his skill of finding digital pictures, Jon Schmitz, historian-archivist, for his suggestions, knowledge and patience and Marlie Bendiksen for her assistance retrieving information.

CWC members who searched for pictures include Jeannette Kahlenberg, Sylvia Faust, Joan Keogh, and Anita Ferguson. Others who helped include Gerry McElree, Meredith Rousseau, Alyce Milks and especially Barbara Vackar. Thank you to Jim Freay for his help copying pictures, Mark Northrup and Victor Northrup for their computer skills and Roger Coda for the use of his 2008 photograph of the CWC members. Many facts, names and anecdotes were taken from the annual notebooks housed at the Chautauqua Women's Club. Most of the photographs in this publication were found in the CWC annual scrapbooks and the Oliver Archives collection. Ann Walsh helped with the historic 1935 White House photograph. The photograph of Susan B. Anthony belongs to member Cathy Bonner, who graciously allowed us to use the portrait. Special appreciation also goes to Denise Marie Fugo for her significant contribution to the on-going history of the Club and the women who contributed their energy and expertise to Chautauqua.

Finally, Dr. E. Dorothy Dann Bullock included the following dedication to her 1974 publication: "This history is dedicated to the consecrated leaders and hundreds of loyal and faithful Chautauqua women who, by their gifts of time, talents and money have made possible the eighty-five year life of the Chautauqua Women's Club." Thirty-five years later, the CWC is thriving due to that same dedication from leaders and members who share, serve, learn and influence others.

Janet Myers Northrup
March 2009

FOUNDING *Women:*
Inspiration and Impact on
Chautauqua and the Nation

II. The Beginning

Not so long ago an advertising jingle reminded women, "You've come a long way, baby." In many ways that ad campaign idea exemplifies the changes at the Chautauqua Women's Club over the past 120 years. When the first Chautauqua lectures were delivered in 1874, women were still forty-five years away from being allowed to vote. The Civil War had ended only nine years earlier and many families still mourned loved ones killed or wounded in battles. At that time the women's programs and lectures at Chautauqua typically included topics such as: missionary work, hygiene, managing the home, rearing children, working with servants, and cooking. Women participants, often as many as 200 people, convened Monday through Friday at 8:00 a.m. By 1879 when the (first) Hall of Philosophy was constructed, women met in that open sided structure because they had no other large space for meetings. Though it is difficult to believe today, one of the Chautauqua founders was reticent to have any woman address the general Assembly, but ladies did speak at the women's meetings. Nevertheless, the Chautauqua Women's Club's (CWC) history is closely linked not only to the Institution's development, but also to growing national movements of the time including Temperance, Suffrage, The League of Nations, The Women's Relief Corps and the National Service School, The National Federation of Women's Clubs and other financial, health and social programs. Under the leadership of twenty CWC Presidents from 1889 to 2009, the group has evolved. As that old ad implies, women at the CWC have come a long way. Now they meet in a well-maintained lake front building that was constructed in 1929 for CWC purposes. While the Chautauqua Women's Club serves a social and educational function and is a support to Chautauqua Institution's programs, today's members also facilitate annual contributions of thousands of dollars to student scholarships in music, dance and art.

The Chautauqua Women's Club building, located at 30 South Lake and Janes Avenue, celebrates eighty years of service to the Chautauqua community in 2009. However, as an organization, the Chautauqua Women's Club is even older, having been established in 1889 as a department of Chautauqua Institution in furthering its goals. An annual report issued in 2002 explains, "This mission is accomplished through funding scholarships, providing opportunities for intellectual endeavors and (offering) an environment for social enjoyment of members." At a time when many groups recruit volunteers with great difficulty, one might ask:

Why and how does the Chautauqua Women's Club continue as a thriving organization?

How and why was the CWC Clubhouse built and how is this eighty-year-old building maintained, especially when the Chautauqua season lasts only nine weeks?

To what extent were CWC members and leaders involved in early political and social movements of the Nineteenth and Twentieth Centuries?

What opportunities does the Club provide for 21st Century women and men? Does the CWC continue to serve as a leader in education?

Why do so many Chautauquans support this organization by their attendance, volunteerism and finances?

Are opportunities made there for younger women or men to serve?

And finally, how does the Chautauqua Women's Club encourage, enrich and support the Chautauqua program?

First and best of all (at Chautauqua) is the Women's Club. Of course, there are Woman's Clubs everywhere. But none of them are like the Chautauqua Woman's Club. One may only suggest rather than try to analyze its charm. It consists, primarily perhaps, in its unique membership of cultured women with the soft tones of the sunny hospitable south on their tongues and the ripened beauty of the Old South in their hearts and lives, of their sisters from all parts of the energetic west and charming east and capable New England... It consists of forward looking programs, the efficient drill of its various activities, its friendships of a life-time, its manifold co-operative activities, the constant inspiration which it radiates not only for the coming year, but for life, the gracious hospitality which clusters about its club house. Little wonder that women find peace and hope and joy here.- George William Gerwig's hand-bound book, *Chautauqua an Appreciation* published by the Roycrofters of East Aurora, NY in 1924.

The Chautauqua Women's Club was built in 1929; the Temperance House is the building on the left in this picture.

When approaching the CWC building on Janes Avenue, two entrances are available, one for any physically challenged visitor entering the dining room and a second one for entering a foyer with stairs. To the right, or west, of the foyer is a dining room with a large table, used for hundreds of planning sessions and social gatherings. The room displays a watercolor of the Clubhouse with a tent erected on the lawn, depicting one of the community-enjoyed Strawberry Festivals. This beautiful watercolor was painted by the artist/member Rita Argen Auerbach and is a reminder of a major annual Club activity. The room also displays a collection of wooden Cat's Meow miniatures of Chautauqua landmarks such as Alumni Hall, the Athenaeum Hotel, Norton Hall and the Children's Fountain. On the wall beyond the central table is a grouping of photographs of women who served as president of the organization. These women lived for the rest of the year in their home states of Florida, Texas, Wisconsin, Iowa, Arizona, Pennsylvania, New York, Illinois, and Colorado. Each of these leaders made lasting contributions to the Club's history and success. Most were involved in national movements. One president was an organizer of the WCTU (Women's Christian Temperance Union) and several others were leaders of the General Federation of Women's Clubs at state or national levels. One worked to establish the League of Nations and another represented the AAUW. Many were suffragists and college educators. These women influenced the activities and advancements made to the organization while they served. According to one of those presidents, Dr. E. Dorothy Dann Bullock, author of the Club's *The History of Eighty-five Years 1889-1974*, "The progenitors are the great women who left their impression on the club and created this heritage…They were 'educated gentle women' who created the image for our club and gave the members a consciousness of the importance of women in educational and national affairs as well as in domestic and social areas."[1] Dr. Bullock also stated there were "...within the membership and scheduled speakers, distinguished women who were the leaders of national movements such as Frances Willard, Jane Addams, Martha Berry, Carrie Chapman Catt and Susan B. Anthony." [2] Two of the earliest leaders were relatives of Chautauqua founders John Heyl Vincent and Lewis Miller.

Turning to the East from the foyer the visitor notices an impressive living room or "gathering space" of the House that is 33' 9" by 38' 3". The fireplace is important because the women who first dreamed of a Women's Club in Chautauqua back in 1902, stipulated "...the assembly room in which the club would hold meetings be made as open as possible, and that it contain a large fireplace"[3] Above this fireplace is an oil portrait of the third club president, Anna Hardwicke Pennybacker (Mrs. Percy V. Pennybacker). In the northwest corner of the room is a Steinway "A" piano, which has a long Chautauqua history and will be discussed later. The Steinway was refurbished in 2007 through the generosity of donors and is used for recitals or events. Several of the other furniture pieces in the room were member donated family heirlooms.

Women celebrating a member's birthday (1940's) in the gathering space

One exits this room through French doors that lead to a comfortable porch overlooking Chautauqua Lake. The porch has two story high ionic columns and is an example of the architectural style known as Southern Colonial Revival.[4] The front lawn of the Clubhouse was enhanced in 2008 when Dr. Sidney Holec presented a special birthday gift to his wife, Anita Van Tassel Holec, in the form of an attractive flower garden with steps and a walkway. The Anita Gardens replaced the sloping lawn shown in the previous House exterior photo and is maintained by volunteers. Commemorative bricks for a patio were sold in 2008 with plans to install an outside patio for entertaining by 2009.

Photo by Abigail S. Fisher

Sidney and Anita Holec in the 2008 garden at the CWC House

Exterior and interior of the Chautauqua Women's Club

Above: The artist's rendition of the House and Strawberry Festival by Rita Argen Auerbach. The Athenaeum Hotel is at the right.   Below: Bridge Instruction occurs

Eleanor Roosevelt (left) spoke at Chautauqua seven times. She is shown here sitting on the CWC porch with President Anna Pennybacker.

Ladies celebrate Thomas Edison's invention at the 1929 Festival of Lights Celebration

Another archival photograph was taken on the porch during the commemoration called "The Festival of Lights" in 1929. The event celebrated Thomas Alva Edison's invention of the incandescent light bulb. The picture shows (l. to r.) Mina Miller Edison, Mrs. Henry Ford, CWC President Anna H. Pennybacker (standing), Mary Miller Nichols, Ann Studebaker Carlisle, and Mrs. Robert Miller. Mina Edison was the wife of the inventor and the daughter of Chautauqua founder Lewis Miller. The lawn of the Athenaeum Hotel is in the background.   *(Photos from the Oliver Archives)*

The Women's Club's neighbor to the North is the 157-room Athenaeum Hotel (built in 1881) and the neighbor to the South is the Frances Willard House, also known formerly as the "Temperance House." This High Victorian multi-peaked structure was purchased in 1925 by Anna Gordon for the WCTU and is one of the most photographed structures on Lake Drive. The building served as the Headquarters of the Temperance Movement for twenty years at Chautauqua and now is privately owned by Kevin and Karen Crowder of Dallas, Texas.

Frances Willard was the first nationally prominent woman to speak at Chautauqua and was also the first President of the WCTU. In her honor, a Tiffany styled window of her likeness was installed in the Anne Kellogg Hall at Chautauqua. Later, the window was moved to the Temperance House. When Chautauqua ceased being the WCTU Headquarters, the window was moved to the new headquarters in Evanston, Illinois.[5] Karen Crowder mentioned that hundreds of Chautauquans may have stopped at the white drinking fountain in front of the "Temperance House" and been cooled by a drink of water before entering the home.[6]

The three neighboring structures of The Athenaeum Hotel, The Chautauqua Women's Club and the Temperance House are important landmarks at the Institution for their architectural beauty, history and location on South Lake Drive.

Frances Willard/ stained glass window

The history of Chautauqua as an experiment (1874) for the training of Sunday school teachers is well documented, but the Chautauqua Lake region was a recreational area long before the Chautauqua Assembly began. The winsome book *Around Chautauqua Lake* quoted an 1874 advertising brochure which stated, "Any one of respectability may come here and spend a few weeks or months at comparatively small cost, not being obliged to follow the dictates of gaudy fashion and costly entertainments in order to be respected."[7] The folder went on to say, "Comfort and pleasure are the ruling passions rather than a desire to display costly trappings, followed by riotous and ruinous dissipation."[8]

The Chautauqua Lake area was accessible as well as respectable. The railroads connected Jamestown, Mayville and Westfield with cities such as Buffalo, Pittsburgh and Cleveland, so the lake was available to many. From the railroad terminals, many visitors took one of the wooden, two or three deck steamers to the Chautauqua Assembly or to other destinations on the lake. Collectively the steamboats were referred to as "the Great White Fleet" and had begun operating on Chautauqua Lake in 1827. By 1898 fourteen steamers traveled the lake daily from the Steamboat Landing in Jamestown to the docks at Mayville on the north end of the lake. The seventeen mile trip took three hours. Jamestown newspapers at the end of the summer of 1907 reported that 280,000 passengers had used the steamers.[9] In fact, one account of the Chautauqua Assembly's first day in 1874 mentions nearly four thousand people from twenty-five states and four countries competed for seats on benches in Miller Park.[10]

The two men behind the Chautauqua Assembly program were Lewis Miller, a wealthy industrialist from Akron, Ohio who invented the Buckeye Reaper, and John Heyl Vincent, a Methodist minister who eventually became Bishop Vincent. The Assembly idea was to train managers and teachers of Sunday Schools to improve religious education in churches. However, the "idea" soon included recreation, non-religious lectures on various topics, a book club called the Chautauqua Literary and Scientific Circle (1878), and a replica of the Holy Lands (1874). The Holy Lands project was, and still is, a teaching device, laid out by Dr. W.W. Wythe, which contains Jerusalem, dozens of towns, Mt. Hermon, the Mediterranean Sea (Chautauqua Lake) and the Dead Sea. Dozens of independent Chautauquas were developed in other states and usually were located in woods or on a lake. As a response to the thirst for education in small town America, the lyceum movement of the 1870's (commercial lecture bureaus) contracted speakers to the Chautauquas such as Mark Twain, Ralph Waldo Emerson, William Jennings Bryan, Susan B. Anthony and P.T. Barnum. Some of those speakers made their way to the original Chautauqua in western New York.

III.

Should Women Be Allowed to Speak at Chautauqua?

Many women participated as audience members in that first session, but few were speakers. An interesting account by Jesse L. Hurlbut (a friend of Chautauqua founders John Heyl Vincent and Lewis Miller) shows the two leaders had different attitudes toward women as speakers. Hurlbut explained, "At every step in the progress of Chautauqua the two founders held frequent consultations. Both belonged to the progressive school of thought, but on some details they differed, and women's sphere was one of their points of disagreement. Miller favored women on the Fair Point platform but Rev. Vincent was in doubt on the subject."[11] Fortunately, Rev. Vincent must have changed his mind regarding women at the podium because in 1876 he consented to have Frances Willard speak prior to a temperance conference.

Frances Willard served as President of Northwestern Female College (1871) and later was named Dean of Women of the Women's College at Northwestern University until resigning her post to become President of the Chicago WCTU and later became National President from 1879 until her death in 1898. Actually, a meeting of the WCTU was held at Chautauqua prior to the first national WCTU convention in Cleveland in November 1874. Frances Willard's address to the Assembly indicates that from the beginning Chautauquans were interested and influential in this national movement.[12] The WCTU was also the first women's organization to draw membership from all levels of society.[13] The 2008 WCTU website credits the organization as "the oldest voluntary nonsectarian woman's organization in continuous existence in the world." Western New York played a prominent role in the cause. Women from nearby Fredonia, New York were the "first of the women's groups to visit saloons, under the leadership of Esther McNeil." The name Women's Christian Temperance Union was adopted on December 22, 1873. During the winter of 1873-74 non-violent vigils were held in Fredonia, Hillsboro, Ohio and Washington Courthouse, Ohio where housewives conducted "pray-ins" at local saloons. Organized women drove liquor from 250 communities in just three months. Some women joined the WCTU as a protest to their own lack of political power since they could not vote, own property or receive child custody when divorce occurred. Many women who became suffragists, gained confidence and learned activist skills in the temperance crusades. The Movement was needed. In the late 1800's, Americans spent over a billion dollars annually on alcoholic beverages, compared with $900 million on meat and less than $200 million on public education. By 1894 the WCTU had expanded its interests to many issues. In fact, in 1896 twenty-five of the thirty departments of their organization did not involve temperance. The WCTU also was one of the first organizations to have a lobbyist in Washington D. C.[14]

The First Women to Address the Assembly and the Early Presidents

Even though Francis Willard was the first prominent woman to speak at the Assembly, other women gave lectures. According to Alfreda Irwin's booklet, *Chautauqua Women's Club History 1889-1989*, at least three other outstanding women were included on the program at the first Chautauqua Sunday School Assembly in 1874. Mrs. W. F. Crafts (the wife of a minister) spoke on "Teaching the Primary Classes." Jennie Fowler Willing, a Professor at Wesleyan University in Illinois (and the wife of a minister), discussed "Women's Work in Sunday School." Willing was a supporter of missionary activities, temperance, and women's roles in public schools.[15] The third speaker was Emily Huntington Miller, sister-in-law of the Chautauqua founder, and the woman who would eventually become the first CWC President. Emily Miller was prominent in the Temperance Movement and Methodist church missionary work.[16] The first four CWC Presidents were Emily Miller, Sarah Vincent, Anna Pennybacker and Jennie Alexander.

Leaders Who Were Founding Women of the CWC

Emily Huntington Miller
1889-1895

Sarah Vincent
1896-1916

Anna Pennybacker
1917-1937

Jennie Alexander
1938

A prior interest united Frances Willard and Emily Huntington Miller as both women were part of a group that started Evanston College for Ladies (the forerunner of Northwestern Female College) where Miss Willard was first President. Miller, who was a writer of children's stories and the editor of a children's magazine, often addressed the Assembly in earlier years.[17] Her lectures in 1877 included the topics "Women's Work in the Church", "The Home as School", and "Our Boys and Girls and Their Work at Home." *The Assembly Herald* newspaper implies she may have spoken at other places on the grounds when it reported, "The Pavilion was too small to hold the masses who gathered at 4:00 Wednesday to hear Mrs. Miller.[18] By 1882, she was directing presentations frequently at Chautauqua on women's lives and their church interests.

The Women's Club Becomes an Official Department of CI

At last in 1889, a watershed year for Chautauqua, the Chautauqua Women's Club was founded as an official department and Emily Huntington Miller was officially designated as the club President. This "designation" came to be the tradition that the Assembly or Institution (as Chautauqua was called under its 1902 charter) would appoint the President of the Chautauqua Women's Club.[19] Apparently after the first meeting, many women gathered at the Lewis Miller house as shown in the archival 1889 photo in this publication. Bishop Vincent addressed the new club and stressed women's responsibility in the home, labeling them the 5 C's—cleanliness, cooking, chemistry, contentment and courtesy.[20] Clearly the programming in the early years concerned the home, missions and temperance. Dr. Vincent wrote a prayer for the CWC meeting in 1900, which "was often used and… valued."[21] The prayer is, "Oh, God, enlighten my mind with truth/ inflame my heart with love/ Inspire my will with courage/

Enrich my life with service/ Sanctify what I am/ Order what I shall be/ And thine shall be the glory and Mine eternal salvation/ Through Jesus Christ, My Lord."

When the CWC began officially at the end of the Nineteenth Century, women's interests were broadening. By 1896 the CWC was affiliated with the General Federation of Women's Clubs. The group became part of the Literary and Educational Organizations of Western New York in 1899 and the State Federation in 1914.[22]

The following picture shows women meeting in the second Hall of Philosophy in 1917. They had met at the first Hall of Philosophy, which was in the same location, during the summers of 1876-1902.

This photo of the Chautauqua Women's Club is dated Aug. 8, 1917

Emily Huntington Miller, the First CWC President

Since most women at Chautauqua in the Nineteenth Century were homemakers, Emily Huntington Miller designed programs on "Woman at Home." Over 200 people gathered at sessions of the CWC held in the Hall of Philosophy. Topics discussed that first year were "house furnishings and decorations, sanitation, hygiene, care and training of children, management of servants, marketing and cooking, dress, social forms and duties and personal improvement.[23]

Historical records indicate in 1878 the grounds had 480 cottages and 234 tents. Dwellings in the Miller Park area were half cottage and half tent structures and a full-season ticket (in 1877) cost $5.00.[24] Meetings of the CWC were held in a formulaic pattern. First, a topic was introduced by a lecture or paper and then the topic was discussed with opinions given by various members.[25] However, growth occurred in women's interests by the end of the century. By 1896 the Assembly's Department of Instruction reported the CWC met twenty-five times, each following the pattern of organization described earlier and including a membership of 125 women with about 400 people attending meetings.[26] They met at 8 a.m., mainly so the women also could attend cooking classes later in the morning. A membership fee of twenty-five cents was collected and used to purchase books on the topics that interested the women.[27] Meetings continued to be held in the Hall of Philosophy as shown in the preceding archival photo from August 8, 1917. The structure took up a full block and was modeled after the Parthenon, but the wooden columns of the first Hall structure were painted to resemble marble. The second Hall of Philosophy, which has sixteen rounded cement columns, replaced the earlier square-pillar structure in 1906.[28] An archival photo from the early 1900's captures the second Hall of Philosophy under construction with a tarp for the roof.

The Chautauqua Woman's Club Holding a Meeting on the Floor of the New Hall of Philosophy

The current Hall of Philosophy under construction in 1903 with a tarp roof

Fortunately, copies of *The Assembly Herald* have been preserved, so we have a record of what transpired at some of the early Chautauqua Women's Club lectures. One address, given by Mary Ashton Livermore on August 22, 1891 in the Hall of Philosophy, shows the passion and style of oratory at the time. Mrs. Livermore was a known speaker who lectured for the Redpath Lyceum Bureau for almost a quarter of a century. She spoke without notes and lectured on various topics such as women's suffrage and temperance. Mrs. Livermore had been an abolitionist, teacher, Editor of *Woman's*

Journal and key organizer of the U.S. Sanitary Commission during the Civil War, an organization that worked to improve health conditions in Northern Army military camps (1861). The *Assembly Herald* described her speech that Chautauqua day as one "which was along the temperance lines (and) was a most eloquent one."

> I want to speak to you of the relation of the liquor traffic to the criminal population of our country. (Here she discussed men who were imprisoned at the Concord Reformatory which housed 850 convicts.) She noted…they are men of intelligence, and in many cases of culture, and yet nine out of every ten came there through either habitual or temporary excess in drink. Almost the entire body of inmates are now organized into a temperance association, and substantial results are accruing…Forty –four of them committed a crime for which they were sentenced because of drink, and have no recollection of the crime.

She then described efforts to "better the condition of women who were imprisoned."

> Ninety-seven per cent of these poor women are brought there through drink. I have visited…thirteen other prisons, and upon the most reliable testimony I assert that eight-tenths of the crime committed in the United States is the direct product of strong drink.
>
> There are five thousand women in the state prisons and penitentiaries of the country and fifty-three thousand men.

> (Reporter) The speaker was emphatic in the demand of better treatment for female convicts, and declared that women of right spirit cannot but regard an insult to one woman as an insult to all women…With vigor Mrs. Livermore attacked criminal immigration and prophesied the overthrow of the rum traffic and universal suffrage in our land. She closed with a description of the rending of mountains by hydraulic pressure, which was both an illustration and prophecy of the annihilation of the saloon.

Editions of the *Chautauqua Assembly Herald* are a valuable source about daily life and issues presented at the Institution. The subscription was $1.00 per Season or four cents per issue. Early accounts of classes for women at Chautauqua always included instruction in cooking. During the 1890's Emma P. Ewing led the popular classes. She was the Director of the Department of Domestic Economy at Purdue University, Principal of the School of Household Science in Kansas City and author of cookbooks. *The Assembly Herald* referred to Ewing as "The first woman to reduce household economy to a system…for training house-keepers" and named her "a most practical, sensible and energetic woman." [29] Emma Ewing gave lectures on "Cookery and

Christianity", "The Cooking of the Future" and "Home Making." Mrs. Ewing addressed the Chautauqua Women's Club frequently.

At a CWC meeting held on August 8, 1890, Emma Ewing read a paper on food preparation. Her cooking philosophy was: "Properly prepared food gives nourishment and strength; improperly prepared food is a fundamental factor in every form of disease…Failure to fit the food to the demands of the body is the cause of untold injury to health and happiness."[30] However, an article in the *Assembly Herald* from July 26, 1890 depicted the appalling conditions of Ewing's teaching environment. The article, written by staff members of the *Herald*, explained they found "something missing at Chautauqua" and then went on to explain,

> In a pouring rain our editorial duties led us past the cooking school tent on Pratt Avenue. The want was not pupils-there were more than there was room for; it was not interest, never had a school a more absorbed and indefatigable body of students; it was not the teacher-there is only one Mrs. Ewing and Chautauqua has got her; it was a respectable housing for this splendid teacher and her school. There they were, pupils and teachers, taking notes, preparing dishes and tempting viands, while across the floor of the tent ran rills of water and off the noses and down the backs of the patient learners trickled streamlets of various sizes. Our appreciation of the department is such that we venture to propose to the management-new quarters for the Cooking school, and may its labors never be less.[31]

One product Emma Ewing recommended was cottolene, a turn-of-the-century lard substitute. Cottolene, an opaque white substance, was sold by the bucket. It had a long shelf-life, needed no refrigeration and was inexpensive, all qualities that women cooking at Chautauqua would appreciate. Advertised as being superior to lard or butter, Cottolene was made by pressing cottonseeds, ninety percent, (abundant in the South) and mixed with ten percent choice beef suet (beef tallow).[32] Mrs. Ewing authored several cookbooks including *Cooking and Castle-Building*, (1880) several small cookery manuals on soups, salads and breads, (1890) and *The Art of Cookery* (1886), which was published by Flood and Vincent at Chautauqua. Mrs. Ewing was kept busy with the cooking classes, sometimes six days a week. The following advertisement for the classes appeared in the *Assembly Herald* during the week of August 10-21, 1891.

Chautauqua Cooking School
1891
Mrs. Emma P. Ewing, Teacher in Charge

Third Course of Lessons

Bread Making, (Free)	Monday, Aug. 10
Broiling,	Tuesday, Aug. 11
Roasting,	Wednesday, Aug. 12
Boiling and Stewing,	Thursday, Aug. 13
Frying,	Friday, Aug. 14
Soups,	Monday, Aug. 17
Salads	Tuesday, Aug. 18
Odds and Ends,	Thursday, Aug. 20
Eggs and omelets	Friday, Aug. 21

Terms
8 lessons $3.20   1 lesson 50 cents
The lesson will begin at 9:30 and close at 10:30 a. m.

Practice Lessons in Bread Making

Tuesdays and Fridays at 8:00 a. m.
One dollar each

The "Practice Bread Making" lesson was held in the Amphitheater so that "all who desire to attend can do so without fear of being crowded."

Advertisements in the 1890 editions of the newspaper also suggest much about life at Chautauqua in the early years. Rooms in cottages rented for three to six dollars per week with "table board found elsewhere." A visitor could rent a small room or a tent at a lower rate. The Athenaeum Hotel ran both American and European plans. Rooms without board were rented for about a dollar per day and upward. Table Board without room was $10.50 per week at that hotel. Stores were also available at the Colonnade and included grocery stores, a bakery, a meat shop and a milk stand. Accounts also mention a candy store, which was a small building conveniently located near the steamboat dock. One ad with a picture printed in the paper touted, "The greatest improvement in corsets during the past twenty years is the use of coralline in the place of horn or whalebone." (Coralline was made from red coral.) Ponds Extract was advertised for mosquito bites and sunburn, while Pears' Soap was recommended for "all who are suffering from fatigue, brain weariness, loss of memory or any form of debility." Imperial Granum was sold as an "extract" recommended for invalids and the aged as well as infants, children, nursing mothers and convalescents. Oxford teachers' Bibles sold for $1.25 and the Remington Standard Typewriter was recommended "for fifteen years the standard, and today the most perfect development of the writing machine." In the early days when streets were unlit, walkers at night needed lanterns. Many roads had roots or stumps, so *The Herald* urged pedestrians "to walk in da middle of da road."

Chautauqua's Assembly Herald, May 1890.
A glimpse of life in the late 1800's; steamships, corsets, and pills to "quickly RESTORE FEMALES to complete Health"!

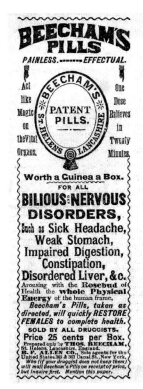

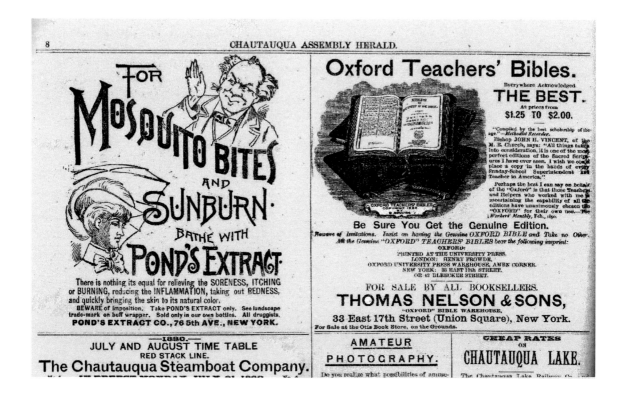

IV.

Where They Lived in the Early Years

The *Assembly Herald* Issue of August 16, 1891 showed similar advertisements to those of 1890, but also offered some different activities for Chautauquans. For example, the Travelers Insurance Company sold an "Insurance Ticket" for twenty-five cents to have someone's "life insured against accident for $3,000" through agent F. H. Farquharson at the C. C. Depot on North Avenue. However, the ad mentioned the caveat, "Ladies Insured Against Death only." A Chautauqua keepsake was sold at the Arcade Building on the Grounds by Jerome R. Graves, the Jeweler. His advertisement explained, "Phillips & Armitage, Jewelers, No. 6 East Third Street, Jamestown, N. Y. have gotten out a souvenir spoon in sterling silver, with profile of Chancellor Vincent and the word 'Chautauqua' on the front of the handle and the Steamboat Landing on the back." One store on the Grounds, operated by Frank Wood, enticed customers to the emporium with the promise of free samples of food. "All lovers of a perfect drink are invited to step into the popular grocery store and get a cup of Van Houten's cocoa. A neat attendant will be on hand to serve all who call…For 77 years this celebrated make has led all others in Europe." No doubt many Chautauqua women took up the offer to sample the cocoa. Another *Assembly Herald* issue advertised "free soup" made by Franco-American, which was available in glass jars or cans at the same store.

Appearing next to the ad for Emma Ewing's Cooking School was the listing about facial blemishes from John H. Woodbury's Dermatological Institute at 125 W. 42nd Street, New York City. "The largest establishment in the world for the treatment of the skin, scalp, eczema, moles, warts, superfluous hair, birthmarks, cancer, hare-lip, moth, freckles, pimples, wrinkles, red nose, red veins, oily skin, acne, blackheads, barber's itch, scars, pitting, powder marks, facial developments, etc.," The ad mentioned "consultation was free at office or by letter. (The) 128 page book on Dermatology and Beauty (was) sent (sealed) for 10 cents."

A six- room cottage with an attic (all plastered) in good condition was for sale including furniture and carpets etc., at 783 Ramble for $1500 and an ad on August 18th offered "Boarding House for sale. Cheap for cash. Enquire at 831 Scott Avenue."

Train excursions were promoted once a week to Bradford, PA to see the Petrolia oil fields in action and a view from a high bridge in that area. Other thrill seekers could visit The Great Rocky Mountain Museum of National History in nearby Lakewood, NY. Major Geo. P. Ryan, Proprietor of the collection, would "…entertain visitors at the Museum with true accounts of his thrilling experiences among the wild animals and savage Indians of the Rockies. Don't fail to see George and his pets", which consisted of Rocky Mountain sheep, live elk and "twenty times more than we advertise."

Most issues of *The Herald* contained a column called "Walks and Talks" which presented some aspect of life at Chautauqua or perhaps an interview with an Amphitheater lecturer. The same issue that presented the previous advertisements also interviewed Julia Ward Howe, the suffragist who wrote the lyrics to "The Battle Hymn of the Republic." Those famous words were published in an 1862 *Atlantic Monthly* and quickly adopted by Union Civil War troops. The reporter concluded, "Mrs. Julia Ward Howe informs me this, her first visit here, has been a pleasant one. She has always been interested in Chautauqua, but has found it to be even more worthy of admiration than she supposed." Howe, the mother of five (surviving) children and wife of the organizer of the Perkins Institute, served as the President of the New England Woman's Club in Boston and was a member of The Woman's Congress, an association for the advancement of women. Curiously, the newspaper did not indicate if Mrs. Howe spent time with the Chautauqua Women's Club although she no doubt did because of the obvious connection with the General Federation of Women's Clubs and suffrage.

4   CHAUTAUQUA ASSEMBLY HERALD.

The Womans' (sic) Club Saturday morning at the Hall of Philosophy was conducted by Mrs. S. M. I. Henry, who introduced the subject, "Prevention of Intemperance," by brief remarks.

Prevention, she said, is infinitely better than reformation, for the memory of impure deeds and vile associations will live. Mrs. Palmer of Wilkes-Barre, presented well-digested thought on the subject. We meet, she said, to talk plans for bettering the individual, plans for reform, social, civil, and national. There is a sweet refrain running through our council, *home, home, home.* Our first thoughts must embrace the fireside. The hope of this and coming generations lies in consecrated and organized womanhood. Let us be vigilant, watching the saloon keeper, remonstrating, expostulating, enforcing the law, distributing literature, elevating public sentiment, organizing children's societies and educating in *scientific temperance.*

Chautauqua Assembly Herald, August, 18, 1890

Cabins, tents and The Longfellow, an early rooming house (Oliver Archives)

The Longfellow on Roberts Avenue was an early rooming house. Many Chautauquans rented or owned either tents or small cabins as shown in the previous photo. Houses at the back of the picture face South Terrace. The Ford and Gale laundry facility and a spring were located behind the building. Other boarding or rooming houses also provided lodging. Some tents were made on the Grounds, but large tents had been purchased at the 1876 Philadelphia World's Fair and brought to Chautauqua.[33] Porches then as now were valued places to socialize, but the tents were used mainly for sleeping and changing of clothing.

Meanwhile, the CWC continued to meet in less than ideal conditions for their needs, one of which was bathroom facilities. At the end of the 1892 Season, Emily Huntington Miller addressed the Assembly. She concluded her speech with a plea to establish a designated building for the CWC meetings rather than the Hall of Philosophy. She stated, "Chautauqua owes woman one thing more. Let her honor herself by building in this coming year of discovery and conquest a noble and beautiful building and inscribe over its door the words, "Woman's Pavilion, 1892" (Applause.) Columbus discovered America. Woman has made it worth living in" (great applause).[34] Unfortunately, the women would have to wait a quarter century before they would have a clubhouse for meetings.

Sarah Elizabeth Vincent Becomes the Second CWC Leader

Emily Miller resigned as leader in 1896 and was replaced by Sarah Elizabeth Vincent, the sister-in-law of Chautauqua founder John Vincent. Mrs. B. T. Vincent served from 1896-1916 and had been Secretary to the organization prior to assuming its leadership. She had also shown leadership as the President of the Pioneer Class (1882) of the Chautauqua Literary and Scientific Circle. Sarah Vincent had been active in the General Federation of Women's Clubs, the New York State Federation and the Western New York chapter. At this time women at CWC meetings often shared what they were doing in their home clubs and the meetings became a place of support for new ideas. On July 21, 1899, the CWC adopted the motto: "One of many and not separate from any."[35] In 1906 the meeting time was changed from 8:00 a.m. to 9:00. Club dues were raised to fifty cents and were used to pay the General and State Federation costs, to support summer school scholarships, to print an annual yearbook and to provide for social functions. Discussion amongst women recognized they needed a permanent structure to hold social functions and to offer restrooms for Assembly visitors.[36]

In 1902 an architect was hired to draw up plans for a clubhouse at Pratt and Ramble, which was estimated to cost $7,500. The women proposed that part of the house should "be kept warm and open during the year."[37] Life memberships were sold for $25 (they issued 300) with the proceeds going toward the House Building Fund. However, the Institution had other uses for the Pratt/Ramble location and the building plans were scrapped. Instead, the money went toward landscaping the lawn below the Hall of Philosophy, which continued to be the open-air meeting place structure for the CWC. The Executive Board gave $500 at Old First Night for the proposed landscaping project "for the beautifying of the entrance Park."[38] Evidence of the planting from that project can be seen today.

A New President: Anna Hardwicke Pennybacker

After leading the CWC for twenty-one years, health issues forced Sarah Vincent to resign from her presidency in 1917. The new Chautauqua President, Dr. Arthur Bestor, appointed Vincent's successor as CWC President, Anna Hardwicke Pennybacker. The new leader was a former history teacher and high school principal from Austin, Texas. Mrs. Pennybacker, who had been active in CWC activities, was a member of the Chautauqua Board of Trustees since 1916 and was the first woman to serve on that Board. Mrs. Pennybacker also had served as Past President of the General Federation of Women's Clubs, a position she relinquished in 1917. During her first year as President of the CWC, the charter was changed to reflect two objectives: self-improvement and mutual helpfulness. Fortunately, Arthur Bestor agreed with Anna Pennybacker and other women that the Chautauqua Women's Club needed a Clubhouse. As a result of this agreement, a committee was formed that was not only dedicated to building a House for the CWC meetings, but also raised $2895.00 for that purpose.[39] Anna Pennybacker was to serve as President from 1917-1937, many of which were difficult financial years for the Institution. She was the first club president who was not related to a Chautauqua founder. Interestingly, Jeanette Bestor, wife of Arthur Bestor, was a member of the Women's Club and their daughter, Mary Frances, would become its leader many years later.

Two Presidents in a typically Chautauqua setting

Anna Pennybacker with Dr. Arthur Bestor,
Chautauqua Institution President 1915-1944

The first Clubhouse 1918

A Building at Last: One Step Forward

The first clubhouse was purchased, not built, between 1917 and 1918. The building was at the corner of Janes and Lake on the site of the current CWC and was a yellow structure "with gingerbread cornices," several porches and an "abundance of full-length windows."[40] Originally the house was called Dean's Cottage. Eventually, it was sold in 1880 to Louis Miller's brother, Jacob Miller, and then to C. D. Firestone in 1895. He sold the house to the Scofields of Warren, Pennsylvania. Dr. Bullock mentioned the time of the CWC purchase was right after World War I. According to Chautauqua County records, home owners Archibald Scofield, his mother and sister sold their leasehold to the women for $8,000/$2,000 down at five percent interest. Remarkably, the loan for this house was paid in full by August 16, 1920 with the final payment coming from WW I U.S. Victory Liberty Bonds. Since money was tight the first year, the women "stripped and painted furniture and made curtains" for the new House.[41] Through their thrift and management the women paid for their house in just three years.

Women's Support for the Troops in World War I
Why Are They Knitting at the Amphitheater?

The effects of World War I were felt strongly at Chautauqua especially in the two summers of 1917 and 1918. Chautauqua President Arthur Bestor was called to Washington to serve as Secretary of the Committee on Patriotism through Education under the National Security League. Addresses in the Amphitheater that year concerned "Mobilizing the Mind of America." [42] Bestor believed by 1918 that "Education had become a means of winning the war."[43] Chautauqua women responded to the war effort and to the programs by joining the National Service School, a branch of which was at Chautauqua on the south side of the Grounds called "The Overlook." Women were billeted there in tents and they learned skills to help the war. The "Commandant" of the National Service School, Mrs. George E. Vincent, was the daughter-in-law of Chautauqua founder John Heyl Vincent. She also belonged to the National League for Woman's Service, which involved driving trainees to a rifle range or youngsters under child welfare programs to centers for health care.[44]

The Service School taught young women how to perform telegraphy and wireless communication. Women's Club records do not indicate how many members were involved in the Service School, but we do know Jeanette Bestor participated by rolling bandages from old sheets for use in dressing wounds. One archival picture shows sewing machines used for making needed supplies. According to her daughter, Mary Frances Bestor Cram, Jeanette Bestor also learned how to run a canteen. Service School women were educated about the effects of the destruction of crops in Europe and "what grains and grinds of grains were most suitable for war-torn countries to utilize in their native bakeries; that fats are fuel for fighters."[45]

Women were given free black wool to crochet black shawls for wounded soldiers. According to one source, "It was during the war years that knitting became common practice during Chautauqua Amphitheater and Hall of Philosophy lectures, a practice that continues to this day." [46] Also, according to Mrs. Cram, "The custom became firmly established, and therefore bore the stamp of approval that only patriotism could have bestowed."[47]

Knitting and sewing for the troops in World War I

Ladies at a flag raising ceremony in Bestor Plaza in front of The Pergola (1917)

Tents at the Overlook (Chautauqua's south end) in 1918

*The Commandant's headquarters: National Service School 1918,
John Heyl Vincent's daughter-in-law, Sarah Elizabeth, served as Commandant.*

Women wore uniforms, drilled in formation and participated in flag lowering ceremonies, sometimes on the commons. (That grassy central park area was named Bestor Plaza after the death of Arthur Bestor in 1944.) The uniform consisted of wearing a white blouse, white tennis shoes and khaki skirt that cost between $1.75 and $2.00. Reveille occurred at 6:00 a.m. and taps at 10:00 p.m. During the day women were involved in calisthenics, classes in food conservation, first aid, dietetics, telegraphy, surgical dressing, typewriting, and Braille.[48] The Red Cross opened an office in the Colonnade building where supplies were accumulated for refugees and hospitals. Also, the *Chautauquan Weekly* published knitting instructions.

V.

Suffragists and Reformers at Chautauqua

Nationally prominent women speakers have always come to Chautauqua, beginning with Frances Willard. In the late 1800's Jane Addams, the financial supporter of the Chicago settlement house, Hull House, addressed the Assembly about her work with immigrants. In that tradition, Chautauqua programming devoted one week, starting July 15, 1918, to Women's Service Week. Addresses in the Amphitheater included CWC President Anna Pennybacker, Suffrage leader Anna Howard Shaw and Carrie Chapman Catt, President of the National Woman's Suffrage Association, who lectured on the topic, "For What Are We Fighting?"[49] Catt, a persuasive speaker, argued that suffrage for women was a patriotic cause, especially during the war and concluded, "You may be working in the Red Cross and knitting socks and sweaters, but you are not doing your part if you fail to do all in your power to support and defend this great issue."[50]

Anna Howard Shaw was the Vice President of the NWSA and, like Catt, a gifted speaker who lectured at Chautauqua. Shaw was a Methodist minister and a medical doctor, but chose instead to work for Women's Suffrage. Anthony's biographer explained that Shaw had been a close associate of Susan B. Anthony until Anthony's death in 1906. In 1882 Miss Anthony had addressed the Chautauqua audience with a stirring oration. As a result, in 1883 John Heyl Vincent invited her back to Chautauqua to debate Suffrage in the Amphitheater with Rev. J. M. Buckley, Editor of *New York Christian Advocate*. Unfortunately, she was too weak after months of traveling to accept the speaking engagement.[51] Anna Shaw participated in the debate instead, but Miss Anthony sat on the Amphitheater stage for support. After the debate, a reception was held for both women and Rev. Buckley in the Hall of Philosophy. We can assume the Women's Club hosted the reception, but no records in the Club show their participation. However, the next day Mr. Buckley concluded, "If any one thing ever has been demonstrated at Chautauqua, by those speeches and all preceding and following them on the same question, it is the sentiment that the vast majority of the people who annually visit this great assembly is in favor of woman suffrage."[52]

Carrie Chapman Catt
National Woman Suffrage Assoc.

Jane Addams, founder Hull House
Bishop John Vincent (left)

Besides the 1918 speeches during Women's Service Week and instruction at the patriotic Service School, other changes also came to Chautauqua that year. For example, admission to the Chautauqua grounds reflected the war effort. The gate fee for an afternoon at Chautauqua was ten cents with an additional penny levied as a "war tax." The evening admission was fifteen cents with two cents war tax. During one lecture Arthur Bestor praised the Chautauqua Traction Company for opening a trolley line from Jamestown past Chautauqua to Mayville and then on to Westfield. Of course this change meant visitors no longer entered the Institution mainly from the steamer dock and virtually changed Chautauqua's front door to the opposite side of the grounds.[53]

VI. Mrs. Pennybacker and Her Friends Enrich the Chautauqua Program

Anna Pennybacker, who served as CWC President from 1917 to 1937, wanted to make the CWC a model club. She had many connections through her efforts in the League of Nations, which resulted in some important speakers at Chautauqua. One speaker was Sir Herbert Ames, former Director of the League of Nations Secretariat, who delivered three lectures.[54] Mrs. Pennybacker was described as "a leader of large capacity and strong personality." [55] She had written the first history textbook for schools in Texas (1885) and was asked to serve as a newspaper correspondent covering the League of Nations Assemblies in Switzerland for Texas newspapers. A *Chautauquan Daily* further described Mrs. Pennybacker as a "suffragette." She knew Carrie Chapman Catt, who had been designated by Susan B. Anthony to lead the group after Miss Anthony stepped down. Mrs. Catt, who was NWSA President when the Nineteenth Amendment was passed, originally had spoken at Chautauqua in 1900. At that time Susan B. Anthony was (again) the featured speaker along with previously mentioned leaders Carrie Chapman Catt and Anna Howard Shaw. More than one hundred years after the speeches by

Anthony, Catt and Shaw, the historic 2008 Presidential contest featured the first serious woman Presidential candidate with Hillary Clinton's bid for the Democratic nomination and Sarah Palin's nomination for the Republican Vice Presidential position.

The candidacies of Hillary Clinton and Sarah Palin should remind people of Susan B. Anthony and others' part in securing the vote for women. On November 5, 1872, Miss Anthony and fourteen other women cast their votes for the Presidential election in Rochester, New York. Anthony, the leader, was arrested at home, handcuffed, tried and fined later at the Courthouse in Canandaigua, New York, but she never served time and did not pay the fine for voting. A New York City newspaper at the time remarked, "This event is henceforth historical, and it will be made the text for hundreds of brilliant orations at coming meetings of the strong-minded."[56] Indeed, Susan B. Anthony's Chautauqua Amphitheater addresses were poignant orations. This leader continued to organize women for the right to vote until her death, but it would take until August 18, 1920 for the Nineteenth Amendment to be ratified. Chautauqua was one of the places where the suffragists campaigned for the vote and the CWC leaders were vocal supporters of the suffrage movement for decades.

Photo courtesy of: Cathy Bonner

Susan B. Anthony

Anna Howard Shaw

Mrs. Pennybacker invited nationally prominent friends to Chautauqua including Lady Aberdeen, the wife of the Governor General of Canada 1893-1898. Lady Aberdeen founded the National Council of Women in Canada (NCWC) in 1893. As noted earlier, Anna Pennybacker also knew Eleanor Roosevelt, who visited Chautauqua for the first time in 1927. [57] Anna Pennybacker introduced Eleanor Roosevelt in the Amphitheater and later presided at a reception at the CWC. (See the earlier photo of Anna Pennybacker and Eleanor Roosevelt on the CWC porch.) A few years earlier, Mrs. Pennybacker had spoken in Carnegie Hall at the memorial service of Eleanor's beloved uncle, Theodore Roosevelt. The service was held a year after the President's death (1919). The friendship had its impact on the whole Club. On January 21, 1935, 903 of the members responded to an invitation to Washington where they were entertained for lunch by the First Lady in the White House. At 2:30 that day, Anna Pennybacker and Eleanor Roosevelt talked on national radio and discussed Chautauqua.[58] According to historian David McCullough's Chautauqua lecture July 1993, Eleanor Roosevelt spoke at Chautauqua seven times.

Anna Pennybacker was responsible for other national activities as well. Under her leadership, 1253 delegates of the General Federation of Women's Clubs attended the group's sixteenth convention that was hosted by Chautauqua June 21-30, 1922. Dr. Bullock mentions over 6,000 people filled the Amphitheater during that gathering. At one of those meetings, Mina Edison, daughter of Lewis Miller, addressed the women delegates and spoke on the history of Chautauqua.[59] The General Federation of Women's Clubs was founded in April 1890 in New York City when sixty-one clubs from around the country formed the organization. The GFWC, chartered by Congress in 1901, is a nondenominational women's volunteer organization. Its purpose is "to support the arts, preserve natural resources, advance education, promote healthy lifestyles, encourage civic involvement and work toward world peace and understanding."[60] The 1922 gathering of the Federation of Women's Clubs raised many concerns for their CWC hosts. Usually the Federation met in cities with many hotels, but at Chautauqua the women needed to be lodged in boarding or rooming houses. The team of organizers decided to inspect all properties where the women would stay. Mary Frances Cram, who was a child at the time, explained:

> At one boarding house that was advertised as having ten double rooms, the inspecting team found they were minimally furnished and clean, but there was only one bathroom on the premises. Not having any real clout in the matter of upgrading facilities, the team found themselves obliged to accept the cheerful assurances of the proprietress that all would be well because "the bathroom is extra large."[61]

Judging from the number of women who attended this conference from all over the country, the meeting was a success in spite of some rooming situations.

One tradition begun during Mrs. Pennybacker's presidency in 1920 was a celebration of CWC members who were seventy-five years of age or older. Jeanette Bestor invited all of those women to the Chautauqua Institution's President's house for an afternoon tea for "The Golden Belles." This gathering was so popular that the tradition of entertaining the women continued for many years at the Bestors' home on Root Avenue.

VII.

Building the Current CWC House in 1929

The 1917-1918 yellow Clubhouse was an improvement for the women from the open-air meetings in the Hall of Philosophy, but the women wanted a home that would be built to serve their needs. As President, Anna Pennybacker established a "Life Membership Plan" of $180 that made construction possible. The $30,000 Georgian-style building (Pennybacker's style choice) was dedicated in 1929 and has been "the Clubhouse" since that time; however, meetings continued to be held at the Hall of Philosophy. The old yellow house was torn down at the end of 1928 and the current house was ready for service by the next year. Fifty years later the Club held a commemorative event to celebrate the construction. At that time (1979), President Dr. E. Dorothy Dann Bullock published a pamphlet about the history of the house. She mentioned the building had been redecorated three times, always through the generosity of the members. That pamphlet also explained an Endowment Fund was started in 1969.[62]

The Chautauqua Women's Club by Rita Argen Auerbach
Front gardens and landscaping were added in 2008.

The 1929 season was spectacular not only for the CWC House construction, but also for the 50th anniversary celebration of Thomas Edison's first incandescent light bulb. Furthermore, 1929 was the hundredth anniversary of Lewis Miller's birth, the construction year of the Chautauqua opera building (Norton Hall), and the organization date of the Chautauqua Symphony Orchestra to play in that hall. In 1930 then New York Governor Franklin Roosevelt and his wife Eleanor revisited the Institution. Dr. John Erskine, first President of Juilliard, spoke in the Amphitheater and aviatrix Amelia Earhart made an appearance after landing her airplane on the golf course. The new CWC building hosted large and small groups all summer. One friend of Anna Pennybacker, artist Violet Oakley, exhibited her pictures of Geneva, Switzerland in the Athenaeum. In 1931, the Chautauqua Women's Club announced a new "poetry contest", which became a tradition that continued until 2006 when the Writers' Center took over this activity. Mrs. John Henry Hammond set up the first awards, which were intended to promote creativity. The first poetry award in 1931 went to Harold Hutcheson, whose father was the head of the Chautauqua piano department. According to Mary Frances Bestor Cram, the poem questions the practice of applauding a performance and whether or not that applause is appropriate. The poem concludes with the lines:

> *The artist finished-paused, his tragic theme*
> *Holding him by its grimmest beauty still*
> *When suddenly there burst forth from the crowd*
> *Noisy applause, shattering music's dream.*
> *Slowly he rose, vain protest curbed by will,*
> *And with his face set immovably, he bowed.*[63]

Surviving the Depression Years

The Depression years of 1933-1937 were times when the CWC and other groups at Chautauqua were involved in fund raising to preserve the Institution. Gate receipts plummeted due to the nation's financial crisis. Fundraisers were necessary as the Institution needed to pay off debt or face the reality that 1936 would be the last year for the programs. At the CWC, Style Shows were held where admission was 10 cents in 1934, 25 cents in 1935 and 35 cents in 1937. A "20" Club was formed where donors gave $50 for benches in the Hall of Philosophy. Dr. Bullock mentioned the role the CWC played in 1936 to save the Institution from financial ruin. The Board of the CWC voted unanimously to assume the obligation of contributing one fifth the assessed valuation of the clubhouse or $2,400 to help decrease the indebtedness incurred during the Depression. Mrs. Pennybacker's appeals to her friends and fellow Chautauquans were put in these words: "Chautauqua stands at the Crossroads; whether it will go on to a glorious triumphant future will be decided to some extent on this Old First Night.[64] According to Jeffrey Simpson's *Chautauqua, An American Utopia*, Anna Pennybacker, "a Texas dowager who directed the Women's Club with an iron fist in a velvet glove" approached John D. Rockefeller, Jr., who gave the remaining $37,000 to pay off Chautauqua's debt on the "next to the last day of the 1936 Season."[65] Chautauqua archivist Jon Schmitz explained that many organizations and individuals contributed to saving Chautauqua. Nevertheless, Rockefeller's generous check was made out not to the Institution, but to the Chautauqua Women's Club and was the dollar amount that took Chautauqua Institution out of debt.[66] One could argue that Anna Pennybacker was the right leader at the right time. She enriched the Chautauqua program by her leadership, friendships with others and dedication.

When Anna Pennybacker died unexpectedly in 1938, finding a replacement was difficult. Finally, the Executive Committee Board prevailed upon a close friend of Mrs. Pennybacker to lead the club for just one year.

Jennie Stuart Wilson Alexander Becomes the Fourth President; Josephine Schain Is the Fifth

Jennie Stuart Wilson Alexander became the fourth President in 1938. Mrs. Alexander had been an active member of the Daughters of the American Revolution and had been a Pennsylvania State Regent (see photo on page 25). Under Mrs. Alexander's leadership the following occurred: a poetry seminar was held for ten days at the Club; ties were strengthened with the General Federation of Women's Clubs; and the Golden Belles were honored with a Club sponsored party. The CWC also served as a "guarantor" of the new Chautauqua Symphony Orchestra.[67] Even though a new leader needed to be chosen to replace Mrs. Alexander's one-year appointment, Eleanor Roosevelt characterized the CWC program that year as "…comprehensive in scope, forceful in appeal, valuable to members of women's clubs everywhere, interesting to everyone…an assembly which is not religious, not a social, not a civic club, but a unique mosaic of all these." [68]

Josephine Schain
5th President
1938-1943

Similar to her predecessors, the new leader, Josephine Schain, was involved with the General Federation Clubs and had been a supporter of the Suffrage Movement. Ms. Schain, the CWC's fifth president (1938-1943), also served as National Director of the Girl Scouts of America 1930-1935, chaired the National Committee on the Cause and Cure of War 1936-1941, was the Director of International Relations in the National League of Women Voters and participated in the International Alliance of Women for Suffrage and Equal Citizenship.

The Women's Club organization turned fifty years old in 1939 and celebrated with a membership dinner at the Athenaeum Hotel. That year the group honored Sadie Orr Dunbar, who was the President of the General Federation of Women's Clubs. During the World War Two years, the CWC worked with the YWCA to raise money for the Allies by sponsoring a gathering at the Bellinger home and sewing for soldiers and refugees. A Hobby Show in 1940 also helped to earn funds to redecorate the House. The CWC held a card party at the Golf Club in 1941 and a bond drive in 1942. The Golden Belle Parties, the Hobby Show and the Poetry Contest were continuing activities from 1939-1943. No style show was held in 1943; however, in 1942 the Art Committee held the first "art exhibit and tea" in the House. This art project was the forerunner to the Chautauqua Art Association. The portrait of Anna Pennybacker was donated to the Club in 1943[69] and currently is hung on the fireplace in the meeting room.

After her death Josephine Schain's personal papers (1886-1972) were donated to Smith College. Those papers show her interest in international peace organizations including The Pan-Pacific Women's Association. Recognized by Smith College with an honorary LL.D degree in 1937, Ms. Schain was described at the time as "a devoted laborer and a valiant and effective leader in the cause of peace, freedom and justice among the peoples of the world."[70] Clearly she was a leader at Chautauqua, nationally and internationally.

Mary Frances Bestor Cram Becomes President

When Josephine Schain resigned in 1943, the trustees appointed a well-known Chautauquan whose father served as President of the Institution. Arthur Bestor died unexpectedly in 1944 after serving as the Chautauqua leader for twenty-nine years. Mary Frances Cram, Bestor's daughter, had grown up at Chautauqua, graduated from Vassar College, taught at Vassar and served as Director of the Chautauqua Recreation Center. She also was an author and lecturer who had worked for CBS.[71] Mary Frances Cram knew Chautauqua thoroughly and claimed to be a "topographical expert" who for years "could not be stumped" about the location of Chautauqua streets, their intersecting streets and the houses, which she associated with the names of original owners and when the homes were built.[72]

Many activities offered during the year of Mrs. Cram's presidency (1944-45) are still enjoyed by CWC members in 2009. These events include: teas, outstanding speakers on national or international affairs, and recitals. Programs often reflected the concerns of the country at war and in 1945 of a country emerging from war.[73] In 1945 the National Federation of Music Clubs held its first annual meeting at Chautauqua and the CWC provided a reception. The National Federation of Music Clubs was founded in 1898 in an effort to coordinate local music clubs throughout the nation and to provide the local clubs with ideas. This music organization has held meetings at the Institution every year since 1945 and was recognized at a July 2008 Chautauqua Symphony Orchestra Concert for over sixty years of Chautauqua participation. The Clubhouse records contain one of the programs from the 1947 meeting of the National Federation of Music Clubs. Dr. E. Dorothy Dann Bullock and other CWC members were involved in this national organization so the meeting was an anticipated event. The Club acquired a Steinway "A" piano that is thought to have belonged to Mrs. Smith-Wilkes.[74] The CWC had the instrument refurbished for recitals played at that 1945 meeting.

Mary Francis Cram
6th President (interim)
1944-1945

Women in the Clubhouse sometime after 1943 when the portrait of Anna Pennybacker was hung in the gathering room.

President Helen Chapman 1946-1953

Helen Chapman, another active officer in the General Federation of Women's Clubs, took over as CWC President when Mary Frances Cram resigned. Helen Chapman had been President of the Illinois Chapter of the General Federation. One of President Chapman's achievements was creating a special group known as the Junior Women's Club (1945) that welcomed younger women, offered relevant programs and provided service opportunities with the main organization.[75] She worked closely with the Institution as it created the Foundation Fund. The financial interest from this program would help in emergencies.[76] The CWC house received attention in the form of redecorating, specifically furniture painting and needlepoint chair seats. The Poetry Contest continued and a writers' group started, which met on Tuesday nights. Dr. Bullock's 1974 history recorded that "In 1948 sixteen men were accepted as Associate Members."[77] From that time on men have been involved in the CWC.

Club officers in 1948 included: Helen Chapman, President; Mrs. S. M. Palmer Honorary Vice President; Vice Presidents: Mrs. A. C. Davis; Mrs. S. M. Hazlett; Mrs. William A. McKnight; Mrs. Christian Weichsel. Secretary was Mrs. Charles McPhail. Treasurer was Mrs. J. C. McKalip. Assistant Treasurer was Mrs. C. F. Troop, Auditor- Mrs. W. W. Snyder and Chaplain- Mrs. D. Truman Stackhouse. "The Council" was the leadership group, now known as the Board of Directors, and consisted of Mrs. Norman Jacobs, Mrs. T. C. Donovan, Mrs. William T. Wood, Mrs. Mary A. B. Ducorran, Mrs.

Russell J. Barrow, Mrs. George C. Williams, Mrs. Edith Duell, Mrs. Julian Richmond, and Mrs. Kenneth Weihe.

According to Alfreda Irwin, growth toward scholarships continued while Helen Chapman served as President. In 1947, for example, the Youth Orchestra received $300 from the CWC. In 1950 a scholarship was presented to Robert Woodside, who later became Chautauqua's Director of Music. In later years he also held other leadership positions at the Institution. Muriel Kirby received the award in 1953; in later years she became the staff pianist at the Chautauqua Music Festival. By the time Helen Chapman left the Presidency, the annual "scholarship giving was nearing $1000."[78]

An article in the 1949 CWC scrapbook mentioned the Club was celebrating its sixtieth year. To honor the occasion, a Hobby Show with sixty exhibitors was arranged by Mrs. Carl Winters and a thousand people attended. The Writing Group had 130 entries for judging that year and a series of workshops was offered with programs on Parliamentary Law, Program Building and Public Welfare. The Club also held three fine art exhibits. The Junior Women's Club "contributed liberally" to the Talent Aid Fund and held a Novelty Auction in the Athenaeum Hotel. Finally, an interesting detail noted in the records that year was the CWC's effort to purchase a cow for Mrs. Aiduk Pahk of Korea in an attempt to aid families. According to the article, the women "collected money enough for two and a half cows."

The Board of Directors of the Women's Club in 1948

Style Shows were popular during the 1940's. The following program from August 24, 1948 featured clothing from two of Jamestown's apparel stores and models from the membership. Names appearing on the cover as fashion models included: Mrs. Arthur Anderson, Mrs. Frederick Cheney, Miss Carol Colton, Mrs. Alfred C. Davis, Mrs. Donald Dame, Miss Sarah Doeright, Miss Mary Dow, Mrs. Benjamin Harris, Mrs. Charles Haskin, Mrs. Dow Kelsey, Mrs. Ralph W. Taylor, Miss Katherine Taylor, Mrs. William Taylor, Mrs. Christian Weichsel, and Mrs. William A. Wood. Other participants were Miss Harriet Howe, Mrs. Helen Freeman and Chairman, Mrs. Lawrence Cornell.

Club Leaders During the 1950's
Lucy Milligan 1954-1958 and Dorothy Houghton 1958-1963

Helen Chapman took a leave of absence as CWC President in 1953 to become President of the General Federation of Women's Clubs.[79] Her successor was Lucy Milligan from New York City. Prior to serving as CWC President, she had been a director of the American Cancer Society Volunteers since 1943. Mrs. Milligan and her husband, organist Harold Milligan, were interested in music. During World War II Lucy Milligan had given "curtain talks" between acts of the Metropolitan Opera productions.

Pres. Helen Chapman
7th President, 1946-1953

Pres. Lucy Milligan
8th President, 1954-1958

Pres. Dorothy Houghton
9th President, 1958-1963

Lucy and Harold Milligan wrote *The Club Members Handbook.* She was known for her "efficiency and graciousness"[80] and an organ scholarship was given in honor of Harold Milligan. Their friend Dorothy Houghton replaced Lucy Milligan as President in 1958. Membership was a priority during the leadership of President Milligan and President Houghton and exceeded 800 members.

Social activities highlighted this time period for the CWC. For example, the Life Membership Party became an annual dinner at the spacious Packard Manor with hostess Mrs. Carl Winters. The group continued to meet there for twenty-five years. The Packard Manor, a well-constructed Tudor home at Chautauqua's north end, had an elevator, house organ, twelve bedrooms and eight bathrooms, imported brick exterior and slate shingles.[81] The Golden Belles were honored at teas and their numbers grew. Activities included: dessert bridge parties, French conversation hours, the poetry contests, style shows, a coffee hour for junior members, renewed interest in Old First Night and a celebration of the Club (seventy years) and the Institution (eighty-five years). In 1959 property owners were encouraged to turn on their lights to recognize such birthdays.[82] Mrs. Houghton, who had been active in the General Federation, was described as having "…boundless enthusiasm and exuberant energy, and was dedicated to Chautauqua ideals and purposes." [83]   Club records from this time contain few pictures and consist mainly of clipped articles from the *Chautauquan Daily* and the *Jamestown Post Journal.*

Many Changes Occur Under the Leadership of Dr. Helen D. Bragdon 1964-1967 and Dr. E. Dorothy Dann Bullock 1967-1989

Up until this time most of the CWC Presidents had been associated with the General Federation of Women's Clubs, often serving as leaders of that national organization. Helen Bragdon, who came from a different background, was the exception. Dr. Bragdon, a graduate of Mount Holyoke College with additional graduate degrees from Harvard University, had been awarded several honorary degrees from other colleges. She had been a professor, college president and from 1948-1963 the General Director of the American Association of University Women (AAUW). The website indicates the purpose of the AAUW is "to promote the importance of education regardless of background or the ability to pay." The AAUW was the result of a merger of three earlier organizations that helped women at the university level at a time when some felt women should not receive higher education. The ACA (Association of Collegiate Alumnae) challenged the writing of a prominent doctor in 1881. At that time Dr. E. H. Clark of Boston, who wrote *Sex in Education*, had argued, "Identical education is a crime before God and humanity that physiology protests against and experience weeps over." The (ACA) women's group wanted to help younger college women to spare them from the discrimination they had faced in universities. The ACA merged with the WACA (Western Association of Collegiate Alumnae) and the SACA (Southern Association) in 1921 thereby founding the AAUW.[84]

Helen Bragdon traveled widely for the AAUW and, as a result, brought in speakers from other countries and various states to the Chautauqua Women's Club. During her presidency Dr. Bragdon encouraged the Flea Market, creative writing, bridge and receptions for new members. Music scholarship aid was increased and the CWC

54

supported the National Federation of Music Clubs. However, the most important advancement during Dr. Bragdon's presidency was a renewal of the Certificate of Incorporation for the CWC. The original charter expired after fifty years. According to Dorothy Dann Bullock, "Such legal procedure was necessary in the State of New York in order that an organization might own property. This project took much time, research, and effort to assure all was in legal order. The new Charter and Certificate of Incorporation is now a perpetual one."[85] Dr. Bragdon's leadership therefore helped the Club with its charter to better serve the Chautauqua community.

Dr. Bullock's Contributions to Music, Scholarships and CWC History

Pres. Helen Bragdon   Pres. E. Dorothy Dann Bullock
1963-1967   1967-1979

As a former President of the National Federation of Music Clubs, Dr. E. Dorothy Dann Bullock supported all interests of the CWC, but was particularly interested in music and scholarships. By the early 1970's CWC scholarships rose to $3880 with an additional $500 given to the student symphony and to their Concert Master. Dr. Bullock was described in "The History of Eighty-five Years 1889-1974" as "eminently qualified educationally and administratively in civic and cultural affairs... along with her dynamic, enthusiastic and friendly personality (she) brought inspiration and 'know how' to the club; and effected a solid growth in club programming and activities, and in service to the Institution."[86]

New Life Members in 1974. Pres. Bullock is third from the right next to Alice and Carl Winters. Frank McElree is at the left.

Dorothy Bullock was a Cornell graduate who received a PhD in music from Elizabethtown College. In 1972 she served as a U. S. delegate to a U.N.E.S.C.O. conference in Paris, appointed by President Nixon. She also had served on the Advisory Committee on the Arts, appointed by President Kennedy.

Articles in Clubhouse scrapbooks from 1969 describe the CWC's decision to establish a Property Endowment Fund in 1969 to "provide for future needs in the care and upkeep of the Women's Club House." The ambitious project was launched under the capable leadership of Mrs. Norman Jacobs. The article describes how the women set a goal for the Centennial year of 1974 by selling decks of playing cards with Chautauqua scenes. They also offered score pads with pictures of the Miller Bell Tower. The Property Endowment Committee consisted of the following: Mrs. Frank McElree, Dr. E. Dorothy Dann Bullock, Mrs. Clyde Carnahan, Miss Helen Estabrook, Mrs. J. W. McCauley, Jr., and Mrs. Nina T. Wensley. At this time and in prior years, women were always listed as their married names appeared, reflecting a more formal time and making research today challenging, as shown by the above list of names.

At the start of the 1967 Season the CWC held a Happy-to-Meet-You-Reception at the Clubhouse. Membership in the Club "is open to both men and women" according to an article that year in the *Chautauquan Daily*. Another activity in the early 1970's involved Lee Chaverin, a professional model, who conducted a visual poise workshop for members of the Morning Group.

Other activities included new member receptions, bridge lessons, "creative writing symposia" and play and poetry contests. Also, an annual series of artist recitals was initiated to benefit the scholarship program.[87] In 1976 a winner of the poetry contest for writers "under 16" was Nancy Gibbs, who eventually became a *Time* Senior Editor in 1991 and Time Editor-at-Large since 2002. She is also a long-time Chautauquan.

Poetry winner Nancy Gibbs (seated in center) age 16 from
"Chautauquan Daily" 1976 - CWC scrapbook

The Language Conversation Hours in the 1970's included Spanish, led by Mrs. George Scofield and Miss Alice Ward and French, led by Mary Mohler. Russian conversation was added in 1971. Gifts were made at the end of the Season to the Chautauqua Fire Department, the Chautauqua Lake Association and prizes for the Bestor Plaza Art Show.

On the 50th Anniversary (1979) the Chautauqua Women's Club received a plaque from the National Register of Historic Places through the Department of the Interior.

Lasting Tradition from the 1976 Berry Festival

The decision was made in the 1970's to offer the Strawberry Festival as a benefit and also as a community service project for people at the Institution. The "Berry Fest" of 1976 was advertised as a place for Chautauquans to meet from 2-4 on the front lawn of the Women's Club where they were served fresh strawberries, ice cream, cake and lemonade to celebrate the nation's Bicentennial celebration. Marguerite Say and Mrs. Hugh Hawthorne headed the committee with assistance from Mrs. Myron G. Johnson and Mrs. Francis Wright. The event has been held yearly since that time.

Another positive development was the report that the Property Endowment Fund had reached $95,000.[88]

Efficient members serving shortcakes at a Strawberry Festival

(above) Mary Cochran and Jean Thurston at a Strawberry Festival. They stand in front of a red and white tent on the lawn of the Women's Club.

During the early 1970's the Junior Club was renamed "The Morning Group" and included social gatherings and programs. In 1973 a pin was designed for Life Members for the first time (see photo on page 66). Another important development occurred in 1973 when the Club discontinued its long association with the General Federation of Women's Clubs because of the by-laws change during Dr. Bullock's Presidency.[89] The Women's Club operates as a nonprofit organization, so the rules under which it operates prevent such affiliations.

Mary Frances Bestor Cram Returns to Presidency in 1980
President Margaret Hasebroock Leads 1980-1982

Pres. Mary Frances Cram
returns in 1980

Pres. Margaret Hasebroock
1980-1982

When Dorothy Dann Bullock resigned in 1979, the Institution appointed Mrs. Mary Frances Bestor Cram, a Chautauqua resident, member of the Chautauqua Board of Trustees and former CWC President to serve again as President until the middle of the 1980 season. Margaret Hasebroock presided for the next two years when the Club was in transition. She was the twelfth woman to serve as president. A 1981 photo in the Club's scrapbooks shows a "Look of the 80's" style show featuring models Lee Chaverin, Kay Logan and Mary Frances Cram. The CWC program, held in Smith-Wilkes Hall, was a benefit for scholarships.

The CWC Board of Directors in 1986

President Marian Clements 1983-1986

Marian Clements came to the CWC Presidency with a different background from the other leaders. Mrs. Clements, a widow, was active in church leadership positions and had been married to a Presbyterian minister. At one point she had served as a Christian missionary in Persia (Iran). Mrs. Clements was a member of the Executive Committee of the National Council of Presbyterian Women and also was a member of their Board of Foreign Missions. She led the CWC in the establishment of a privately endowed scholarship fund through the Club to benefit more student scholarships. According to Alfreda Irwin, the Scholarship Fund added a separate Scholarship Treasurer for "better management of funds" that came from private donors, recitals, and twenty per cent of benefit proceeds.[90] The Scholarship Committee, headed by Beverly Dame Esch, at this time donated around $13,500.

Pres. Marian Clements
1983-1986

During Marian Clements' Presidency, the Morning Group met twice each week, as did bridge instruction. Susan Luehrs, who served as Chairman of the Morning Group, announced varied programs, such as 1) the wife of Chautauqua Institution's President, 2) a make-up artist, and 3) a hostess from the Wensley House. (CWC member Nina T. Wensley donated her lakeside home to the Institution in 1966 to house speakers and special guests.) Dr. Helen Overs, SUNY Fredonia Dean of Women, was the first hostess at Wensley House. Dr. Overs, who served on various CWC committees, initiated and directed the "55 Plus" program at the Institution.

Beverly Dame Esch welcomes student scholarship winners to a picnic

At this time German was added as a fourth language at the weekly Language Hour.[91] The Writers' Symposium and Poetry Contest were popular activities. One featured speaker at the CWC's weekly Writers Symposium in 1985 was Alfreda Irwin, the eighteen-year former editor of the *Chautauquan Daily*, beginning in 1966. Mrs. Irwin had visited Chautauqua since childhood and worked on Chautauqua history and other publications. Several Chautauqua publications were dedicated to her, which honored not only her vast knowledge of the Institution but also her willingness to share that information with others. Alfreda Irwin was honored as an inductee to the National Women's Hall of Fame in Seneca Falls, New York and received other recognitions.

Alfreda Irwin

Also, at this time the CWC's Writers' Center was developed further by Mary Jane Irion; the program was designed to give others the opportunity to improve their writing.

Several photos in this publication show CWC activities in the 1980's. Mary Cochran and Jean Thurston are shown at the Berry Festival, which later was moved to Bestor Plaza and expanded. The 1983 Flea Market with volunteers is shown below. A 1986 picture shows the Property Endowment Committee that organized the Antiques Show, held in the Hall of Christ. Vendors came from New York, Ohio, Pennsylvania and the $2 admission donation went toward the Property Endowment Committee.

Seventeen volunteers at the a "Flea Market" in 1983

The Antiques Show in 1986

Below: Some members of the Property Endowment Committee in 1986: Gerry McElree, Aggie Fausnaugh, Geneva Cherry, Caroline Keating, Jane Lahey and Sylvia Faust (organizers of the Antiques Show). At the right are some CWC Yearbooks.

The CWC Board of Directors in 1985

(Names in alphabetical order): Marian Clements (President), Ruth Bailey, Toni Branch, Ecky Broad, Clary Burgwardt, Dorothy Clark, Geneva Cherry, Mary Cochran, Betty Corwin, Evelyn Davidson, Beverly Esch, Helen Estabrook, Sylvia Faust, Celia Fay, Mary Handley, Jane Hawthorne, Mary Jane Irion, Helen Jacobs, Marjorie Jenkins, Elinor Johnson, Diane Johnson, Joan Keogh, Maxine Lowe, Alyce Milks, Mary Mohler, Marian Neubauer, Norma Putnam, Gwen Read, Francesca Rappole, Jane Ann Schludecker, Deborah Siskind, Marian Stranburg, Mildred Underwood, Mary Louise Viehe, Alice Winters, Bernetha Wright.

Above: Three who served as Chairs of the CWC Flea Markets (2006 photo);
(l. to r.) Lynne Ballard, Marianne Karslake, Rita Redfern.

Three Presidents in Two Years: Meredith Rousseau Tapped in 1987, Dorothy B. Clark (acting 1988) and Margaret Arnold August 1988

Club leadership was in transition once again in the late 1980's, but Mrs. Irwin concluded that "Committees functioned well and the Club enjoyed another good year."[92] One highlight in 1988 was the Amphitheater lecture by Supreme Court Justice Sandra Day O'Connor. President Margaret Arnold, who served as president for just one month, was seated on the stage to represent the Women's Club when the first female Supreme Court Justice spoke at the Institution. Unfortunately, the Club records had no pictures of her. Following the lecture the CWC hosted a reception at the House and named Justice O'Connor an Honorary Life Member.

Pres. Meredith Rousseau
1987; 1992-2001

Dorothy B. Clark
Acting President 1988

Pres. Carolyn Markowski
1989-1991

An event was held on August 10, 1987 honoring Helen Jacobs, who had been a CWC member for over sixty years. As a girl she remembered serving at teas and receptions. Helen was the Club's Recording Secretary for twenty years, Property Endowment Chairman for seventeen years, House Chairman for ten years and member of the Finance Committee for ten years. Helen Jacobs was the daughter of Samuel Hazlett, former President of Chautauqua Institution. Helen understood the necessity of planning and providing for future generations and saw the Property Endowment Fund rise from $1000 to more than $70,000 during the time of her service. The Club expressed its gratitude to Helen for her service and friendship at a reception. Helen Jacobs is a fine example of the volunteer spirit, which so many CWC members have for this organization. She was later named "Director Emerita" in 1997.

Helen Jacobs, active CWC member for over sixty years

Life Member Pin

VIII.

The Centennial Year Is Celebrated
Carolyn Markowski is President 1989-1991

When the Chautauqua Women's Club celebrated its centennial year in 1989, the organization was thriving and providing opportunities for Chautauquans to share, serve and learn. Carolyn Osgood Markowski served as President, the seventeenth woman to be in that leadership role. Three projects marked the centennial remembrance of the CWC. The first was the publication of Alfreda Locke Irwin's booklet, *Chautauqua Women's Club History 1889-1989*, which was distributed to members in 1990. The second activity was collecting portraits of past CWC Presidents whose archival pictures were labeled and hung in the Clubhouse dining room. The third project arranged for the microfilming of all CWC minutes, scrapbooks and yearbooks through SUNY Fredonia. That effort, coordinated by Women's Club History Chair Gwen Read, insured the historical preservation of club records with easy accessibility at the college. All three activities showed how the CWC members were proud of their organization and its history from Miller to Markowski. The year also meant the Clubhouse was sixty years old and steadily in need of more attention and repairs.

Club activities continued the practices started in previous years. For example, by 1990 the annual scholarship awards had increased to $16,100. The number of bridge tables averaged fourteen and weekly foreign language conversations continued in four languages (Spanish, French, German, and either Russian or Swedish). Diana Bower has coordinated the language hour since that time. The "Golden Girls' Tea" was a new event honoring women who had contributed to the club, but who were now retired from committees. The event was similar to the "Golden Belles" receptions of the 1920's, which honored women who were age seventy-five or older. Membership that year included 433 people. The annual Strawberry Festival was held, but the committee now used previously frozen berries to save the women's time and energy. As in former years, music performances were popular including six faculty artist recitals, five voice student programs and fifteen instrumental presentations. President Carolyn Markowski and a committee hosted a reception for new members, which included Amphitheater speaker David Eisenhower, and his wife, Julie Nixon Eisenhower. The Eisenhowers' grandfather was former U.S. President Dwight D. Eisenhower and her father was former President Richard M. Nixon.

A series of Eastman Kodak travelogues had started in 1987 and continued with success. John and Mary Ann McCabe coordinated popular programs on Malaysia, Russia, East African Safari, Israel and the Red Sea and "A Day in the Life of China." The $2.00 per person donation provided the "seed money" for the formation of the CWC Program Endowment Fund. This Program Endowment Fund was supplemented through 2007 from Life Membership fees. A percentage of those fees were later used for Contemporary Issues speaker's costs. Other fundraisers for music scholarships that year included the offer of rugs and bracelet type watches available at the Kopper Korner and Athenaeum Hotel.

Club records for 1990 and subsequent years reveal upgrades and maintenance of the building every year. The group financially responsible for this upkeep is the Property Endowment Committee, which approves and supports annual and long range needs while using five to seven percent of the income from the Property Endowment Fund for capital improvements. The House Committee made repairs on the roof and gutters in 1987.

By 1991 Club membership dipped to 298, but the CWC still managed to provide $17,200 in scholarships. Enjoyable activities included more travelogues, the Flea Market, Bridge Instruction, the Antique Show, The Thrift Shop and hospitality teas. For the first time in the Club's history, twice weekly CWC Hall of Philosophy lectures were taped. Those tapes became part of the Chautauqua lecture series. CWC members enjoyed another new activity for many by participating in a Japanese tea ceremony, a special event held at Smith-Wilkes Hall.

The House Committee was busy as well. They purchased new wicker chairs for the CWC porch and decisions were made for redecorating the bedrooms in 1992. Further planning was developed for a "Season's Greetings" party to welcome people at the start of the 1992 season. That hospitality activity, held the first week of the season, had been known as "Happy to Meet You" during the 1960's.

Meredith Rousseau Picks Up the Gavel Again, 1992-2001

Chautauqua President Dan Bratton tapped Meredith C. Rousseau to succeed Marian Clements as CWC leader in 1987. Ms. Rousseau brought her experience as an instructor in English and Public Speaking at Pennsylvania State University, York to the position. Meredith Rousseau received her Bachelor's and Master's degrees from the University of Wisconsin. A two-year experience as a guide at the United Nations Headquarters and a year of study at the College of Europe in Bruges, Belgium, deepened her interest in international and multicultural affairs. Unfortunately, health concerns prevented her return as President in 1988, but she was invited to resume the presidency in 1992 through 2001. During an interview with this writer in 2008, Meredith Rousseau discussed her management style and goals for the CWC. She explained she planned to make the Women's Club "as humanly open as possible" and wanted the organization to be welcoming to all.

Efforts were made to increase the membership, which stood at 254. Working with Membership Chair Pat Stine, CWC membership doubled and included men and women. One successful idea was Ms. Rousseau's decision to encourage younger women and short-term Chautauquans to participate in CWC functions. As a result, nearly one hundred new women attended the first "Morning Coffee" activity in 1992. Ms. Rousseau is proud of the leadership and instruction made in the Writers' Center (then a part of the CWC) under the expert guidance of Mary Jean Irion.

A significant contribution was a program prepared by Mary Boenke and Lin Winters in the Hall of Philosophy on the subject of justice for gay and transgendered people. The topic had never been discussed at Chautauqua, but four hundred people attended and no protests occurred. Parents and Friends of Lesbians and Gays (Pflag), which had found no place to meet on the Grounds, approached the Women's Club with a request to meet in the House living room, which was approved by the Board with no dissent. Pflag continues to offer support and compassion at the Women's Club at noon on Thursdays. The CWC program was an early attempt at educating others when sponsoring such programs meant taking a risk.[93] The Women in Ministry group also requested weekly meeting space and subsequently became a regular feature on the CWC calendar through 2007.

The House Committee made some important decisions during Ms. Rousseau's presidency. The committee decided to have vinyl siding installed to the exterior of the CWC and to tune the 1880 Steinway "A" piano. Another important addition was the purchase of an answering machine. Discussions were also held to make the dining room accessible to all.

Three Women's Club Presidents

Mary Kunze   Barbara Vackar   Meredith Rousseau

Many successes occurred in 1992. For example, the scholarship fund increased again, this time to $18,200. A large contributor to this fund was the financially successful annual Flea Market. That year the Property Endowment Committee offered "Cat's Meow" miniatures including a Chautauqua street sign, a sailboat, a lamppost and the Athenaeum Hotel. Travelogues, always a popular activity, were offered including Hawaii, Yosemite, Bangkok and China. New programs and fundraising opportunities were added. Program Chairs Jane Lahey and Mary Ann McCabe suggested that the twice-weekly lectures in the Hall of Philosophy should focus on "contemporary" issues. Thus began the annual seventeen lectures as an addendum to the Chautauqua calendar in the form of the Contemporary Issues Forum. These lectures did not necessarily follow the Chautauqua weekly theme, but provided the participants with a different opportunity for learning. Clearly Chautauquans were interested to hear outstanding speakers tackle modern problems. One example was Julia Alvarez, author, poet and U. N. Ambassador from the Dominican Republic, who spoke about "The Old in the New World" to an enthusiastic group of people.

Jane Lahey   CI President Dan Bratton   Mary Ann McCabe

The Club offered popular catered pasta suppers as a fundraiser and served 667 people at the House in 1992. By 1993 a new informative Women's Club brochure was printed, scholarships increased to $18,350, bridge instruction was up to thirty-six tables and Club membership grew to 323 by early August.

The Clubhouse, as usual, needed some upgrades. As a result, The House Committee replaced screens, painted shutters and windows and repaired the sidewalk of the Janes entrance.

A new fundraiser of the Property Endowment Committee was the offer of twenty Cat's Meow handcrafted miniatures of Chautauqua landmarks, a popular tradition that continued until 2005. The Chautauqua miniatures were made from a seven-step process that included sanding, screen-painting and hand finishing. According to the CWC Yearbook, "The Property Endowment Committee was established in 1969 to insure the proper care and maintenance of the Club House. Income from the Endowment is used for capital improvements, beautification, and emergency repairs."

*Cat's Meow Miniatures of the Athenaeum Hotel
and Episcopal Chapel*

As a result of fund raising activities from the whole Club, $19,300 was donated to "The Chautauqua Fund" for scholarships in 1994. The CWC Yearbook explains that the Scholarship Endowment Fund "…was established… to help provide for the continuance of the CWC's extensive scholarship program. In addition to income from investments, this endowment sponsors the 'Phantom Ball' and accepts private donor gifts to fund either long-term or one-year scholarships." Chair Marjorie Kemper concluded, "Like the Scholarship Fund, the Scholarship Endowment Fund receives a percentage of some of the club's benefit receipts. Whereas the Scholarship Fund gets 20% of the many CWC benefits and 25% of the Crafters' proceeds, the Endowment usually is awarded 5% of the club's benefits."[94]

Marjorie Kemper explained, "The Scholarship Endowment Fund was created in August of 1996 and re-affirmed in July of 1997 with Anita Ferguson as chairman. The fund accepts and invests donor gifts of stock and cash. Donors can be honored with named scholarships."[95] Many sources contribute to the fund. For example, The Flea Market, under Chair Lynne Ballard, made large financial contributions to the Scholarship Fund. Wink Gasser and Debi Clementi organized the pasta suppers, which originated at the CWC but were later held at the Gallery (restaurant) in the St. Elmo. The Club offered a poster by Gloria Plevin titled "My Garden in Summer with Delphiniums." Rita Auerbach donated another painting for sale, "Chautauqua Montage." The money for scholarships was derived from the effort of many volunteers and continues to be a major activity for some members. Mrs. Kemper mentioned the "trustees report the value of the fund to the Scholarship Committee and a percentage of the endowment is given to the Scholarship Fund each year."[96] Scholarship Committee members enjoyed working on the Club's fundraisers, which included the Flea Market, Flea Boutique, Strawberry Festival and various activities during the year.

Betty Horne chaired the creative writing classes in 1994 and Beverly Dame Esch arranged thirty recitals. That year the CWC considered printing a newsletter during the winter, elected Elinor Johnson Director Emerita of the Club and improved the House with the addition of a new porch awning. Unfortunately, the Club received the sad news of the passing of Ruth Bailey, who had served as the House Chair. Ruth Bailey served as Treasurer for more than thirty years, according to Joan Keogh. Ruth's mother, Nina Wensley, also had been CWC Treasurer. Ruth went on to be a member of the Property Endowment Committee, where she was the Treasurer, starting in 1964.

Beverly Dame Esch showed continued enthusiasm as Chair of the Scholarship Committee, reaching $20,000 in contributions for the first time in 1995. The Committee arranged a well-received annual pot-luck picnic at the Clubhouse. This special early Season event allowed scholarship students, their teachers and private donors to meet each other on an informal basis.

As previously noted, in 1995 two organizations, Pflag and the Women in Ministry Group, received permission to use the CWC for meetings. Also the YWCA of Jamestown rented the House for a luncheon following the address by U. S. Supreme Court Justice Sandra Day O'Connor.

Frequently in the 1990's the often-used building received necessary improvements. For example, a new furnace was installed on the third floor. "Collar ties" were added to stabilize the shifting at the front of the building where the porch was separating from the house. Of special interest was the addition (finally) of a "rented computer" at the CWC for the first time.

Other activities continued at the CWC and new ones were added. The Strawberry Festival raised its price by offering shortcakes for $2.50. The Property Endowment Committee offered Cat's Meow replicas of Kellogg Hall and the Episcopal Chapel. The CWC donated yard goods and bedspreads that were converted into costumes for ballets such as "Spartacus" and others. The Thrift Shop changed its name to the "Thrift Boutique." Fundraisers in 1995 also included the popular Antique Sale and the Flea Market.

In 1995 the portrait of former President Anna Pennybacker was cleaned, restored and hung above the fireplace. Financially the Club was doing well. The membership reached 550-600 by the end of the Season, which was double the membership from three years earlier. As a result of increased membership, a decision was made to establish a CWC Savings Account "to be used to fund some type of outreach program for the good of Chautauqua, whenever possible."

Lectures at the club-sponsored "Contemporary Issues Forum" in the Hall of Philosophy included, "Women in Politics: Does It Make a Difference?" by Honorable Jane Campbell, State Representative from Cleveland and "Domestic Justice: The Hard Part" given by NYS Supreme Court Judge Carolyn Demarest. The Contemporary Issues Forums held each Wednesday and Saturday proved to be a great educational success. Highlights of the 1996 program included the following topics amongst the speeches: "Election '96: Can the Clintons Do It Again?" by Jack Nelson, Chief Washington Correspondent for the Los Angeles Times; "It's Not How Old You Are: It's How Old Your Immune System Is" by Dr. Bruce Rabin (1022 attended this lecture); "The Press: What Can We Expect in the 21st Century?" by Nancy Woodhull, Founding Editor of *USA Today.*

CWC membership increased and Membership Chair Pat Stine reported 526 on the roster in 1996. Over all, the database included 1262 names. The CWC continued to introduce younger women to the Club with an offer of cappuccino on the deck of the Refectory as one activity.

The pasta suppers of previous years had been successful fundraisers, contributing about a third of the scholarship money. However, when the Gallery was closed in 1996, the CWC devised another highly successful concept. "The Evening of Gourmet Dining" evolved into "Guess Who's Coming to Dinner?" The evening consisted of hors d'oeuvres, door prizes, a silent auction and dinner at Chautauquans' homes, which was followed by dessert in the parlor of the Athenaeum Hotel. This fundraiser was so popular that it sold out and netted over $9,000.

Lynne Ballard and Marianne Karslake were praised as Chairs of the successful annual Flea Market. That year Rita Auerbach's watercolor of the 1996 Strawberry Festival was presented to the Board and hung in the CWC dining room. The painting depicts a tent set up in front of the CWC House for the Festival on the lawn and is shown earlier in this book.

The Season's Greetings Committee hosted the welcome to Chautauqua reception in late June 1997. Membership was over 660 for the year with 1323 in the database. Discussion was started that year about three celebrations coming up in 1999, which showed how the milestone year was anticipated for the 125th anniversary of Chautauqua Institution, the 110th Anniversary of the CWC and the 70th anniversary of the CWC House.

The Property Endowment Committee members discussed three fundraisers at the start of the 1997 season. First, a volunteer solicitation would be made to raise money for the House. Second, the Cat's Meow buildings offered that year would be the Colonnade building, the rear view of the Hall of Philosophy and the Children's Fountain in front of the post office. Third, the Antique Show would be held at the Hall of Christ. Scholarships in 1997 jumped to $24,850 and, as noted previously, the Scholarship Endowment Committee was created.

Committees in 1997, which continue into 2009, provide many ways for members to participate in CWC activities. These committees include: Scholarship Endowment, Finance, Flea Market, House, Language Hour, Program Endowment, Property Endowment, Life Membership, History, Nominating, Publicity, Programs, Scholarships and Recitals. Each of these committees has a chairperson and numerous other people committed to the activity.

One important event in 1997 was the Western New York Federation of Women's Clubs convention held at Chautauqua Institution May 20-22. International President Faye Z. Dissinger spoke at the Hall of Philosophy. At that convention the GFWC encouraged the Chautauqua Women's Club to rejoin the parent organization, but the rewritten charter from the 1980's does not allow the affiliation.

The Contemporary Issues Forum lectures in 1997 offered some educational speeches such as: "Who Owns Your Body?" by Madeleine Pelner Cosman PhD, JD; and "The Suffragettes: Leadership Models for the 21st Century" by Judge Linda Ludgate. The Forum also hosted an international Colloquium on U. S. Cuba Relations involving a dialogue between representatives from Cuba and Washington, D. C.

The Strawberry Festival, guided by Chair Jean Wilson, served 1062 and included a musical trio, volunteers wearing Victorian costumes, balloon sculptures, storytelling, a maypole dance, face painting, and Das Puppenspeil (puppet show). The festival was moved from the CWC lawn to Bestor Plaza this season. Some ladies in Victorian clothing are shown on the next page.

"Wink" Gasser   Ann Lehman   Mary Ritts   Rita Auerbach   Diane Hess

Highlights of 1997 included nominating Dorothy Clark as Director Emerita and publishing the first "off-season newsletter." Debi Clementi was the newsletter Editor. Member Mary Ritts offered a generous gift that year to install a gas fireplace and logs in the living room at the CWC. She is one of the participants in the previous photograph.

Keeping track of membership was an arduous task due to changes of names, addresses and enrollment, now at an estimated 1500 people. Naomi Kaufman started the computerization of membership files in 1997. Donna Russell (Registrar) continued to bring the files up to date and then converted the information to computer disks in 1998. In subsequent years Grace Ferguson Zarou created a website for the CWC which was linked with the Institution. Jeannette Kahlenberg later took over the Registrar's position, where she continues to maintain the records with expertise. Another technological improvement was the purchase of a laptop computer for Treasurer MJ Albert that same year.

The Flea Market (Marianne Karslake and Lynne Ballard served as Chairs) was once more the CWC's biggest fundraiser, reaching $11,546.78 in 1997. The best of the Flea Market "leftovers" were saved for a weekly thrift shop, which generated more funds for the CWC and scholarships. The thrift shop location was (and still is) behind the Colonnade building. The Antique Show had success as well that year. The organizers had twenty-one dealers and 600 patrons in 1997 and 648 attendees in 1998. The CWC craft sales were held at the Farmers' Market every Tuesday and Thursday with about twelve vendors per week. These crafters sell beautiful items they have made and then donate 25% of their earnings. Because of the artistry of their products, eventually they renamed their artists' group "Artists at the Market" in the summer of 2008. Bridge instruction was offered and netted $922 for the year. Sylvia Waller was the Chair and in 1998 that group raised $868. Beverly Dame Esch's committee announced $25,970 would be available for scholarships and forty-four recitals were scheduled.

The Flea Market behind the Colonnade Building in 2002

Program Chairs Jane Lahey and Mary Ann McCabe were commended again for the excellence of the Contemporary Issues Forum. Lectures in 1997 included "Political Violence and Terrorism in the Middle East" by Bard E. O'Neill, Director of Middle East Studies at National War College and "Madame President: An Insider's View of How Women Are Changing Politics" by Eleanor Clift, Contributing Editor *Newsweek Magazine.*

Another success was the Strawberry Festival. Jean Wilson, Chair, announced 1156 people were served in two hours at a rate of approximately one person per second. Her committee used 66 tubs of strawberries, 1100 biscuits, 27 workers (most in Victorian dresses) and youth volunteers, who received a free movie ticket to the Cinema from owner Paul Schmidt. The profit was $1639, but according to Wilson the real profit is the "incalculable good will." The Strawberry Festival is considered to be a CWC gift to the Chautauqua community.

Preparations for Chautauqua's 125th season were evident throughout the previous season. The CWC considered holding the following activities: two teas, offering a commemorative Chautauqua umbrella and producing a video: "An Historical Perspective of the Changing Positions and Traditions of Women in America for Over 125 Years."

Meanwhile, other activities and recognitions continued. For example, John Clark was offered a Life Membership to the CWC for his volunteer efforts to the Club projects. Pat Stine organized the skit and song for Old First Night, "Chautauqua Banana" performance in the Amphitheater.

Women's Club routine at an Old First Night celebration

Also of note was the offering of Cat's Meow Creations, with this year's selections being a sailboat and a miniature of Alumni Hall.

125TH Anniversary Year: 1999

This season was one of celebration and recognition for the 125 years since the founding of Chautauqua Institution. Appropriately so, Beverly Dame Esch was given a CWC Life Membership award. Through her committee's efforts, $26,900 in scholarships was awarded at Old First Night in 1999. Forty-seven recitals were presented and forty-six students received music scholarships that year. Certificates of Appreciation were presented to Deborah First and Laura Damon for writing and presenting their program, "Ladies, Learners and Leaders" which was converted into a video. This program was an overview of women's influence and contributions to Chautauqua since its inception.

The CWC contributed to the 125th Anniversary Time Capsule with such items as the year's CWC button and life pin, a prediction about Chautauqua life in 2049, three copies of CWC songs and a picture of the Board. The Time Capsule was an old safe used by Dr. Theodore Flood (the former Publisher of *The Chautauquan* magazine and *The Assembly Herald*, the forerunner of the *Chautauquan Daily*) in the late 1800's. The safe with items contributed from several groups was on display in Smith Library throughout 1999 and will be opened in fifty years.

One new activity that year for the CWC was "The Gift of the Heart" program. According to Chair Marianne Karslake, volunteers assembled ninety-three baby and school kits for a Kosovo Relief Project. Also $255 was donated to Church World Service. Another activity was a (sold out) Victorian tea, an intergenerational experience attended by 150 in the Athenaeum parlor. Nancy Levine, Joan Keogh and the entire committee were commended for the tea's great success.

The House received some additional care in this special year as well. House Chair Joan Keogh reported the front porch pillar bases had been refurbished and in 1999 a winter canvas covering the front porch was installed. Flea Market volunteers were pleased with the new canopies that were purchased as sun protection for the event. Judy Cornell was in charge of the Thrift Shop. In addition to the Strawberry Festival, the women made the decision to offer strawberry jam. Carole Reeder contacted the Kraft Company, which subsequently contributed two cases of Certo and 2000 recipes for making jam. Numerous quarts were made and then served in one-ounce paper containers. Carole Reeder, who was Membership Chair, sewed thirty aprons for the praised event. Her husband, Bob Reeder, often made repairs to the House, which everyone appreciated.

The Contemporary Issues Forum offered interesting choices in the anniversary year. As of 1992 the Forum published a brochure listing the topics and speakers of all seventeen lectures. Some of these presentations were: "Ladies, Learners and Leaders" by CWC members Deborah First and Laura Damon; "Irving Berlin: A Daughter Remembers" by Damaris Peters Pike; and "The Theology of the Hammer" by Millard Fuller, Founder, President Habitat for Humanity.

The House also received a necessary update for this special year. The House has five bedrooms on the second floor, which are rented during the Season. The House Committee arranged to have two bathrooms redecorated, painted the hallway and repaired a ceiling. The CWC offered an anniversary silver spoon, which displayed a picture of the bell tower and the date 1874-1999. The order for this item sold out quickly. Two new Cat's Meow additions were the Lewis Miller cottage and the 1874 Miller tent. Many members participated in the annual dinner with speaker Jeffrey Simpson, author of *Chautauqua, the Real Story*.

Looking forward to the next year, Scholarship Committee Members made plans for a "Phantom Ball" for 2000, the proceeds going to the Endowment Fund. At this event donations would be converted into tickets for a drawing of prizes, but an actual "ball" would not take place. Donna Russell, Elisabeth Groninger and John Clark obtained information for the annual yearbook published by the CWC and distributed in the spring. The Officers in 1999 included Maureen O'Connor Rovegno, Recording Secretary, Andrea Zarou, Chaplain, and M. J. Albert, Treasurer. Finance Committee Chair Angie Twist, explained and presented the annual budget.

Unfortunately, the year brought sad news of the death of E. Dorothy Dann Bullock, who had served as CWC President from 1968-1979.

Celebrating the Memorable White House Luncheon

Meredith Rousseau continued to lead the club for her tenth year in 2000. The year marked the sixty-fifth anniversary of the Club's 1935 lunch at the White House with Eleanor Roosevelt. To commemorate that luncheon in 2000, a tea was held while June Miller Spann presented a history of that enjoyable day. The women learned of the 1700 women invited to the White House, 903 CWC members attended. Also, June Spann noted *The Washington Post*'s report (January 22, 1935) that the White House guests were served "ham, potato salad, buns, pickles, coffee, ice cream and cake." (see photo page 99)

Another success of 2000 was the "Phantom Ball," which raised over $10,000. That year the Strawberry Festival served 1301 people. The Cat's Meow building for the year was the Smith Memorial Library and the Antique Show, also a success, had 699 attend. Talks began with the Institution about the location of the Flea Market. CI offered three bus garages near the Turner Center as a potential site, but CWC organizers preferred to keep the sale in the existing location behind the Colonnade.

Chautauquans continued to enjoy the Contemporary Issues Series. A sampling of the lectures included the following topics: "The Environment and Humanitarian Challenges of Our World at Six Billion" by Julia Taft, Assistant Secretary of State for Population, Refugees and Migration; and "Education for the New Millennium: A British Perspective" by William Glover, Academic Director of Brighton (UK) College School of Excellence.

The annual brochure for these lectures reminded everyone that the Contemporary Issues Forum evolved from the first formal meeting of the Chautauqua Women's Club held July 25, 1889 in the Hall of Philosophy with Mrs. Emily Huntington Miller presiding.

President Mary Monsen Kunze 2002-2004

Membership reached 978 and a new Club President was welcomed in 2002. Mary Monsen Kunze from Elm Grove, Wisconsin, served in the leadership role for three years. Dr. Kunze, a graduate of Northwestern's Kellogg School of Management, earned an MS in Bioethics and later finished her PhD studies (Bioethics) in Italy. She explained, "My goal as President was to honor our long tradition while bringing programs to the Contemporary Issues Forum that invigorated our audiences."[97] Several honors occurred during the season. A reception was held for retiring President Meredith Rousseau and Life Memberships were given to Hella and Scott McVay, CI President. Beverly Dame Esch announced the CWC was listed as "Top Giver" in the Chautauqua Fund. Fifty-two music recitals were scheduled, including a performance by the New Arts Trio in Lenna Hall, and a record of $36,725 was donated for scholarships.

Improvements at the House included a new stove for the kitchen, carpeting for the upstairs hall and bedrooms and ceiling fans. Filing cabinets and a desk were added to the President's office. A new assessment of properties occurred that year for tax purposes and the CWC was assessed at $715,000. Donna Russell worked on the CWC website and the Board continued to update communication. Those who built the House in 1929 would be pleasantly surprised by the new assessment from the original construction cost of $30,000 as well as the advancements in communication technology.

Pres. Mary Monsen Kunze
2002-2004

Meanwhile, the Young Women's Group, reorganized in 2000, initiated fundraising projects. That year the women decided their donations would be going to the Children's School for scholarships.

Members of the Young Women's Group in the Clubhouse
Front row: Beth Gilpin, Cheryl Rolley, Jo Ann Raynow Schaus, Lynn Stonaker.
Back row: Chris Milks, Susan Alexander, Barbara Hois.

As always, the Contemporary Issues Forum topics brought enthusiastic participation. Three of the topics were: "Supreme Court Justice and Nuremberg Prosecutor Robert H. Jackson" by Prof. John Q. Barrett; "Trickle Up in China" by

Mildred Robbins Leet, Founder of Trickle Up; and "The Model for Presidential Ethics: Harry S. Truman" by John Sisley.

At the Club Maram Hijazi, a Palestinian visiting Chautauqua who lived in Israel's Neve Shalom/Wahat al Salam, made an informal presentation about positive relationships and life in her town. Another activity was an outreach effort of the CWC to the Woman's Self-Care Center in Jamestown, a cottage industry selling crafts. The House was reassessed at $782,500, which meant additional insurance premium costs. During the season the CWC worked on changes to the Amendments to the By-Laws. A resolution was passed on use of the CWC facility limiting activities of outside groups as a result of increased use by Club events. Other projects involved discussion on appropriating space for bicycle parking on Janes Avenue and adding a handicapped accessibility ramp from the dining area to the gathering space. Two other new committees were established, an Old First Night Committee and a Cutting Garden Group. Another decision was made to mail the yearbooks starting in 2003. The Women's Club donated $500 to the Chautauqua Lake Association. Members also participated in a Chautauqua community celebration called the "William and Giuseppe Street Fair" in conjunction with The Friends of the Theatre, Friends of the Opera and the Center for the Visual Arts.

Contemporary Issues speakers in 2002 included Lynn Sherr from ABC News, Helen Leary, professional genealogist, Leroy Hopkins, expert on the Underground Railroad and Adrian Morrison speaking on "The Necessity of Using Animals in Research."

A record number of scholarships were contributed to the music, art, theater and dance students in 2003. The Strawberry Festival engaged sixty-two volunteers and The Flea Boutique and Flea Market brought in $8,474. Contributions were made to the Chautauqua Watershed Conservancy, The Chautauqua Fire Department, and The Chautauqua Lake Association.

A Victorian Tea "Celebrating Us" (birthday celebration) was held in 2002 for members and included a sing-along of Cole Porter songs. Also, forty-two recitals were scheduled. The new web page was linked to the Chautauqua web page, intended to improve organization and communication.

Other developments occurred with an Antiques Show and Clubhouse maintenance in 2002. The Antique Show moved to the Turner Building and had twenty-five dealers. Also participating was Vivian Highberg, who assessed antiques for the PBS program, "The Antiques Road Show." A new kitchen floor was installed at the House, the porch was "redone," and new silver chests were purchased.

Communication Advances and a Celebration of 75 Years

Communication improvements were a priority in 2003. As a result, the CWC formed a Publicity Committee to coordinate efforts including the yearbooks, *Chautauquan Daily* communication, kiosks on the red brick walk, a CWC newsletter, the calendar and the fall, winter and spring editions of *Chautauquan*. In addition, a new spreadsheet program was implemented for CWC finances. Fortunately, the House purchased a microphone and amplifier for use in activities.

The popular Contemporary Issues Forum, under the leadership of Elisabeth Groninger and Mary Ann McCabe, included presentations in 2003 on "Femenomics: Women, Worth and Work" by Catherine Ingrassia, Asst. Professor Virginia Commonwealth University; "Death, Dying and the Ethic of Lamentation" by Carlos Gomez, Medical Director Palliative Care University of Virginia; "Leadership Lessons Learned in the Space Program" by Astronaut Susan J. Helms (veteran of five space flights), "Live Wires" Public and Private Risk in Our Lives Online" by Senior CNN Producer Waits May and "The Secret to End Hunger" by Catherine Bertini, Director of the World Food Bank.

The CWC celebrated the seventy-fifth anniversary of the House in 2004 with the "Hats On" birthday party with those attending asked to wear a birthday hat of some type. Members also were pleased to see facility improvements made by the House Committee. A celebration occurred at the "Season's Greetings" welcome when President Mary Kunze honored Marianne Karslake for her dedication, organization and work at the Flea Market.

Mary Monsen Kunze   Marianne Karslake   Dick Karslake

An enjoyable event of 2004 was a welcoming tea for Jane Becker, as Chautauqua's new First Lady. That year the Young Women's Group planned other activities. They worked at the Strawberry Festival and arranged for a gathering of themselves and children at Midway Park during the season. As usual, the Poetry Contest held a reading of the winning submissions and awarded prizes on August 19th under the Chair of Jean Badger. As noted, poetry contests had been held at the CWC since 1931.

Another new event was the Chautauqua Artistry Silent Auction, sponsored as an activity by the Property Endowment Committee. Gerry McElree, long time Chair of Property Endowment, had more jobs to do with her committee as the Clubhouse aged. The Silent Auction offered dozens of donated wooden items, all with Chautauqua themes, (bird houses, plaques, furniture) which were displayed at the Hultquist Center for several days and then offered to people through bidding. Proceeds from this event went to the Property Endowment Fund.

The year brought successes and new challenges. Debate continued throughout the summer regarding the proposed location of the Flea Market and Flea Boutique. These two events, essential elements of CWC fundraising, brought in around $25,000 annually. Four women agreed to chair the Flea Market in 2005, Elissa Terry, Rita Redfern, Marianne Karslake and Lynne Ballard. The Institution once again offered the bus garage at the Turner Center as an alternative site, but the CWC decided the bus garage provided inadequate winter storage, no sun protection and reduced convenience to the Central Chautauqua location. Organizers recognized a need of guidelines for donated items toward this important, but time-consuming activity.

The Strawberry Festival added new entertainment that year with lawn bowling and croquet. Victorian dresses were stored at the House and could be borrowed by CWC members who participated at the Strawberry Festival. Unfortunately, at the end of the season, President Mary Kunze resigned to take another position. As a result, Mary Ann McCabe agreed to serve as Interim President while a national search was made for a new leader.

Interim President Mary Ann McCabe 2004-2005

Mary Ann McCabe, from Rochester, New York, was the nineteenth woman to serve as Club President. Although she had a background in speech pathology, Mrs. McCabe had served in leadership positions in the AAUW, Friends of the Women's Rights National Park (at Seneca Falls, NY) and the Rochester International Friendship Council, which helps international students adjust to university life in America. She founded the Hospital Volunteer Interpreter Program for all Rochester hospitals where 137 interpreters, who spoke fifty-seven languages and dialects, were used for communication in medical situations. Mary Ann McCabe had been an active member of the CWC for twenty years, instituted the Kodak travel films at the Institution with her husband John McCabe, and helped co-chair the Contemporary Issues Lectures Series since its inception. She had a thorough knowledge of the Club's organization, personnel and activities and was an ideal choice for the leadership position.

Mary Ann Mc Cabe, Interim
President 2004-2005

The Contemporary Issues Forum, led by Program Chair Dianne Foglesong and President Mary Ann McCabe, planned seventeen lectures including, "Director's View: American Theatre Today" by Kim Rubenstein; "Marshall Plan and Iraq Reconstruction" by Prof. Jerry Pops; "Interfaith Dialogue on Jewish Meditation, Mysticism, and Alternative Healing" by Rabbi David Zeller; and "Henry Clay Frick and the Inner Meaning of His Art Collection" by Margaret Sangor Frick, great granddaughter of the industrialist.

Barbara Ellison Vackar Becomes CWC President in 2005

At the start of the 2005 Season, Barbara Ellison Vackar, from Austin, Texas, brought a unique set of skills and experiences to the Presidency of the CWC. Her professional and organizational experiences included Special Assistant to the White House under the Carter Administration, Director of Catering for the University of Texas, and Director of Special Events for the Office of the President of the University of Texas at Austin.

In the business community Barbara was President and owner of Adams Vackar Caterers, founded a cooperative government relations and business development strategy firm as well as being part owner of Vackar Development, which planned and designed growth properties in Austin. Barbara demonstrated her leadership abilities in the many community service positions she held including the National Women's History Museum in Dallas, Leadership Austin, the National Women's Political Caucus, Planned Parenthood, The League of Women Voters, and founder of the Austin Women's Network. She established the Austin Consumer Credit Counseling Services for Child and Family Services.

Barbara Vackar
President since 2005

As Good Will Ambassador for the City of Austin, Barbara hosted delegations from Sister Cities and traveled to four countries on trade missions. She was an AARP Texas lobbyist, Coordinator of the Texas Equal Rights Amendment, and elected as the Democratic County Chair in Austin. She also served on boards of numerous non-profit organizations. Barbara Vackar received awards including the honor of "Outstanding

Young Woman of America" and "The Women in Communication Award for Outstanding Community Service."

The Board determined three areas of focus for the CWC in 2005: scholarships, program and property. That year a "conditions assessment" of the Clubhouse was made. Johnson-Smith and Associates (preservation architectural firm) in coordination with the Women's Club Property Endowment Committee concluded the building was in good shape, but would need a new roof soon. The assessment also determined twenty-five other areas in the house and grounds that were in need of attention. Tibb Middleton, another Texan, served as the new House Manager.

Scholarship assistance reached new heights in 2005. Fifty-six students received financial aid when the CWC provided $43,575 for scholarships. Jean Wilson chaired the annual welcoming picnic for the scholarship students and their teachers, an event that is always appreciated.

Each year various Chautauqua organizations present checks at Chautauqua's birthday party, also known as "Old First Night." In 2005 several Club members participated in the Old First Night skit to the tune of "Hey, Big Spender," which was directed by member Dottie Clark. Participants shown in the 2005 photo were (left to right): *Bev Meer, Dianne Hussey, Dottie Clark, Barbara Vackar, Rita Argen Auerbach, Marilyn Ciancio, Frances Rubin, and Ann Fletcher.*

"Hey, Big Spender" CWC Old First Night skit"

Plans were implemented for redecorating the building and refurbishing the Steinway piano as part of the House Beautification Project. According to Club member Anita Ferguson, the 1880 Steinway "A" instrument was donated to the Institution in the 1940's by Annie Wilkes (Mrs. Smith-Wilkes). Mary Frances Bestor Cram, Club President at that time, arranged to purchase the piano for $100, which was then moved (from the Jamestown YWCA) to the House. This piano had been renovated and used at the first meeting of the National Federation of Music Clubs in the 1940's. Anita Ferguson described the National Federation of Music Clubs' meeting as a "big event." She explained, "Unfortunately, age is not favorable to pianos because the instruments are basically machines with moving parts."[98] As a result, Mrs. Ferguson concluded the "Dowager" piano (which is six feet long and has eighty-five keys) was in bad condition again by 2005. After debate about whether or not to repair the instrument, three benefactors came forward, each donating a large sum of money. Through a connection with the Steinway Company of New York City that company generously agreed to pay half of the cost of renovating this historic piano inside and outside. Other contributors donated additional funds to transport the piano to and from New York and purchased an adjustable artists bench.

Barbara Vackar (left) with donors Ann Weber, Bob Fletcher, Josette Rolley and the 1880 historic Steinway "A" piano

Moving the piano for a complete renovation (2006)

At the Season's Greeting event in June 2007, plans were made to unveil the Steinway and dedicate the artists' bench to Beverly Dame Esch in honor of the commitment she showed to the Scholarship Committee and students. Decisions also were made to move the piano to a humidity and temperature-controlled environment in the "off season."[99] However, by 2008, the alternative idea was to "wrap" the piano for the cold months and to leave the instrument in the house as moving a piano is costly.

The Steinway was signed after the renovation in 2006

At the end of the 2006 summer Beverly Dame Esch resigned from the Scholarship Committee after serving as the Chair for twenty-five years. Mrs. Esch announced seventy students received scholarships that year, amounting to $83,875. The Scholarship Committee consisted of thirty-three members and hosted about forty-five recitals each summer. Recipients included students in the schools of music, art theatre and dance. Beverly Esch became involved with student scholarships in 1977 when she responded to a request for financial aid for a piano student. At that time the CWC came up with $50 donation for that student and the scholarship fund has grown since then.[100]

*CI Pres. Tom Becker honors
Beverly Dame Esch for her service*

IX.

The Brown-Giffin Lecture Is Established
Some Changes to Program Endowment and the Writers Center

The CWC Contemporary Issues Forum received a generous $60,000 gift to the Program Endowment Fund in memory of Daisy and Paul Brown of Missouri in 2006. A result of this gift was the establishment of a named lecture each summer. In 2007 The Brown-Giffin Lecture was presented by retired U. S. Supreme Court Justice Sandra Day O'Connor. In 2008 the speaker was Jane Pauley, former NBC journalist and "Today Show" host. Author Gail Sheehy was the scheduled speaker for the lecture in 2009.

Some of the Contemporary Issues lectures in 2006, under Chairs Dianne Foglesong and President Barbara Vackar, were: "Who's in Control? Medicine and Morals at the End of Life" by Dr. Hunter Groninger, Medical Director Capital Hospice Washington; "See Jane Hit: Aggression in the New American Girl" by Dr. Jim Garbarino, Cornell University; "Identity Theft: From Consumer Basics to Hot Topic" by Attorney Joanne Crane; and "Capturing Our Time Through History" by Haynes Johnson, Pulitzer Prize-winning journalist.

A CHAUTAUQUA CONVERSATION

with Retired

JUSTICE SANDRA DAY O'CONNOR

Chautauqua Women's Club   *President Barbara Vackar*   *August 9, 2007*

Some young Chautauqua women were invited to a conversation with former U. S Supreme Court Justice Sandra Day O'Connor at the Clubhouse 8/9/07 following the first Brown-Giffin Lecture

Another change in the program in 2006 was a decision regarding the Poetry Contest. Two members who had chaired the CWC contest were Francesca Rappole and later Jean Badger. The Writers' Center made the offer to manage the Poetry Contest rather than the CWC. This decision for change brought much discussion since the CWC had offered either poetry contests or writing instruction since 1931. A new program, a discussion group that had started in 2005 and was facilitated by John Khosh, evolved in 2006 into "The Week in Review," coordinated by Cathy Bonner. Another new group was the Koffee Klub for those members who had been active participants over a period of years. The group's purpose was to discuss the roles of women today. The "Charity Knit In" was initiated, an activity where women created scarves and items for charitable gifts, reminiscent of the knitting that women had done back in 1918 in the Amphitheater. Eleanor Haupt McKnight led a support group called "Griefshare." Another development in 2006 was the creation of a new Club website that facilitated communication amongst the membership.

The second Brown-Giffin Lecture in 2008, given by Jane Pauley
Left to right in the picture are Dianne Foglesong, Don and Esther Giffin,
Jane Pauley, Mary and Max Brown and Barbara Vackar.

The Scholarship Committee announced a record amount available for scholarships, according to the 2006 "Newsletter." Activities included the Flea Market, Flea Boutique, Antique Show Strawberry Festival, Meet and Greet and Craft Fair. The latter group, mentioned earlier, sells crafts made by CWC members and other crafters with donations going toward the CWC Scholarship Fund. Lucille Piper and Hope Alcorn co-chair the Craft Sales.

Other CWC activities involved the volunteer efforts of many members. The Entrée Who? project was successful in 2006 with proceeds roughly $20,000. Before the event, Judy Cornell offered a decorative quilt for the silent auction, which was purchased and donated to the Oliver Archives. The themed quilt was made from old tee shirts that advertised events at Chautauqua including golf, tennis, opera, theater, the Old First Night Run and others. A new publicity item in 2006 was a tri-fold informational brochure about the club. The building received attention too. Discussion took place about adding AV equipment, which eventually was donated by the Men's Group to the House. The Men's Group uses the Women's Club for their meetings every Friday.

The "French Maids" served at the successful "Entre Who?" project at The CWC.
Left to right are Cheryl Rolley, Dottie Clark, Mary Jane Shank, Rita Argen Auerbach,
Rene Schecter, and Josette Rolley

That year the House Committee added newly reupholstered club furniture fabricated by Wellman Brothers of Jamestown. The CWC made contributions to several organizations in addition to the scholarship contributions. For example, recipients in 2006 included: the Bell Tower Scholarship, the Chautauqua Fire Department, the Chautauqua Lake Association, Hospice, Chautauqua Watershed, and the Chautauqua Foundation. Some people say the Women's Club accomplishes more in the nine weeks of the Season than many organizations accomplish in a year.

Judy Cornell with her donated
Chautauqua quilt before the
"Entre Who?" project in 2006

X.

Taking Care of the House

Even with a positive assessment of the Clubhouse, certain problems needed to be addressed in 2007 and 2008. Joan Keogh, the dedicated House Chairman since 1993, reported finding carpenter ants in one of the front pillars, so that structural work had to be done. Another major repair in 2007 was the house roof replacement completed by Mayshark Builders, Inc. As Chairperson, Joan Keogh shared some of the Committee's accomplishments in the recent years. For example, in 2002-2003, the Janes Street entrance received a "complete overhaul." She explained, "old cement was removed, new concrete was poured, ramps both to the new bike area and to the dining room were built. New planting areas were also added to beautify the area." She said the Property Endowment Committee paid for all but $7,000 of the upgrades, with the remainder coming from the CWC treasury. The House Committee also found it necessary to raise the room rates by $35 and increase the "hostess salaries…to $1700 each.[101]

The Season's Greetings Committee in August 2007
Front: Susan Bonsignore, Dottie Clark, Ann Fletcher, Jo-An Webb
Back: Carole Reiss, Margaret Worden, Margaret Bethea, and Diane Hussey

One of the pillars damaged by carpenter ants in 2007

Property Endowment Committee 2007

Row 1 seated- Chair Alyce Milks; row 2- Carole Griffiths, Sylvia Faust, Barbara Vackar, Pat Rowe; row 3- Aggie Fausnaugh, Molly Reinhart, Carole Glowe, Marian Stranburg, Gerry McElree, Helen Snyder; back row- Josette Rolley, Bette Keane, Dianne Martin, Patricia Dietly, and Joan Keogh.

The Property Endowment Committee considered applying for grants to renovate the building, even though the House is an historical site. However, certain past renovations disqualify such applications. During 2007 President Barbara Vackar called a meeting for members to draw up a "wish list" regarding maintenance and restoration of the Clubhouse. Some of the items under discussion included handicapped bathrooms, electrical upgrades, an interior ramp, kitchen upgrade, laundry facilities, outdoor hospitality area, ceiling fans and an outdoor speaker system. The House Committee was divided into four units with members working in each area. These include: Structural/Interior (Ann Fletcher); Landscaping (Betsy Martin); Grants (Cathy Bonner and Renee Schecter); and Operations (Darlene Huron, Dick Meer, Diane Hussey and Margaret Bethea). Joan Keogh resigned as House Chair (as of 2008) and Darlene Huron and Josette Rolley took over this important position as House Committee Co-Chairs. One of the suggested improvements, an outside hospitality area, was addressed in 2008 with the sale of Friendship Bricks. Anyone could donate a brick with an imprinted name of an honoree, which would then be placed in a new brick patio at the front of the building. Ann Fletcher made an appeal to the membership at the 2008 Life Member Luncheon to give generously toward the house renovations and updates.

Pat Hirt and Diane Hussey organized the Friendship Brick sale in
2008 for the installation of the new patio in 2009.

(left) Comedian Mark Russell and Rita Argen Auerbach entertain as Mark learns how to paint.

(right) singer Kenneth Anderson, the Steinway, and Anita Ferguson after the tribute to Paul Robeson (2007).

Student scholarship benefactors Hale and Judy Oliver enjoy the Life Membership Lunch at the Athenaeum Hotel in 2008. Judy has served on the CWC Board of Directors.

In 2007 and 2008 the organization enjoyed some special educational opportunities. One was Sandra Day O'Connor's address in the Amphitheater. Later, the CWC provided an opportunity for several girls from age 15-22 to meet with Justice O'Connor in a unique mentoring session. Another event celebrated the life of member Mary Ritts, who had been an early TV puppeteer and artist. Mary had lived at the house during the summer and often participated in CWC functions with her friend and fellow pianist, Dee Heinzerling. The "Memory session" in her honor, also involved the Ritts family. A successful musical event held in 2007 involved Kenneth Anderson, a singer who performed a tribute to Paul Robeson with over 250 people attending. Member Anita Ferguson accompanied Mr. Anderson on the renovated Steinway piano. Member Audre Bunis helped set up an original event in 2007 which involved artist Rita Argen Auerbach and satirist entertainer Mark Russell.

Suzanne Brandon and Chris Milks
(Strawberry Festival organizers)

Anita Ferguson
(member/pianist)

Rita instructed the popular humorist how to paint a picture, which later was auctioned. Chautauquan Van McConnon donated the venue and food for this successful Club fundraiser. Paul Anthony was the event's Master of Ceremonies. Another popular offering for CWC members was the "Thursday Morning Coffee," led in 2008 by Virginia DiPucci, Lindsay Weidner and Beverley Meer. This program invited a Chautauqua person to speak on a topic of his or her expertise and offered much variety and insight. Dale and Howard Sanders hosted the "Morning Coffee" at 9:15 on Thursdays for several years. The Sanders provided cake to accompany the coffee and tea. Although the cake is no longer offered, audiences continue to pour in. One program presented by Chautauquan Herb Keyser (in 2006) highlighted "The Life and Music of Jerome Kern, Richard Rogers and Oscar Hammerstein." In another program Chautauqua President Tom Becker discussed the London Conference of the Abrahamic Program. Director Vivienne Benesch spoke on "Serving the Chautauqua Community and the Larger American Theatre." In 2007 pianist Rebecca Pennys discussed "The Chautauqua School of Music" and (Hotel Manager) Bruce Stanton informed everyone about the "Past, Present and Future of the Athenaeum Hotel." Patricia McBride Bonnefoux enlightened the group about the "Chautauqua Ballet Company and School of Dance." In 2008 the speakers included Greg Prechtl (Boys and Girls Club), Tom Wineman (Institutional flower arranger), and Dick Karslake (The History and Operation of the CLSC.) Those who attended the lectures learned a lot about the inner workings of Chautauqua and enjoyed some outstanding presentations.

Mah Jongg was another activity (besides bridge instruction) that attracted players. Mah Jongg, taught by Darlene Huron, was offered Sunday evening and one other day each week. Also in 2007 the Koffe Klub started on Wednesday mornings with a "guided discussion" led by one member. Several participants in this group had been part of the "original" Thursday Morning Group.

The Club invented unique fund-raisers and opportunities every year. For example, The Property Endowment Committee offered an opportunity in 2008 for "Celebrity Doodles" which were auctioned, each coming from an athlete, actor, musician, artist or other celebrity. The "doodles" were displayed at the Hultquist Center, so Chautauquans could view the drawings ahead of time. The Phantom Ball Committee would (NOT) hold the Phantom Ball in December 2008. The Property Endowment Committee offered a round plate in 2007 and an oval one in 2008, both from the Bemus Point Pottery. The popular plates had "Chautauqua" lettered in blue and also depicted sailboats and the historic Miller Bell Tower.

Members were generous with their volunteer hours. In 2007 scholarships were given amounting to $87,675 and by 2008 reached over $100,750.00. All members were encouraged to participate in activities; as a result, the committees included so many names that would be too numerous to record here. However, each year a "Yearbook" is printed that records committee leaders and those who serve. Grace Ferguson Zarou maintained the website in 2006-07, secured funding for the Yearbook through local merchants and was in charge of printing this important booklet, which contains names of nearly 700 members, with addresses and contact information. The CWC library retains some of the earliest Yearbooks, which began in 1901. The decision was made in 2008 to publish *Founding Women,* a book intended to commemorate the Chautauqua Women's

Club's 120-year birthday (est.1889), the 80th anniversary of the House (built in 1929) and 135 years of women meeting at Chautauqua (since 1874).

The Contemporary Issues Forum offered several lectures in 2008. Rosemarie Hidalgo-McCabe, from the National Latin Alliance for the Elimination of Domestic Violence, spoke on "Social Action to End Domestic Violence"; Robert Foglesong PhD, President of MSU and a retired Four Star General discussed "Developing Leaders for the 21st Century"; and Jane Pauley, newscaster/journalist gave the Brown-Giffin Lecture on "Talking About Mental Illness: How Being Bipolar Has Affected My Life."

PIANIST ALEXANDER GAVRYLYUK 2007

THEN AND NOW:
Alexander Gavrylyuk used the CWC Steinway (1880) to practice before performing in the Amphitheater. On the wall behind the piano is a picture of the CWC women in the White House on the occasion of the historic lunch with "First Lady" Eleanor Roosevelt (1935). Mrs. Roosevelt extended an invitation to the Chautauqua Women's Club for a visit to the White House, but apparently was surprised when 903 women arrived. The photo on the next page shows the crowded, but memorable gathering.

A section of the White House photo; the actual photo measures 9.5" tall x 36" long.

Anna Pennybacker is front row third from left and Eleanor Roosevelt is standing next to her. Chautauqua President Arthur Bestor and League of Voters President Carrie Chapman Catt also attended. The buffet lunch was served in the State Dining Room and the guests moved to the Green, Red and Blue Rooms with their plates, allowing space for others. The CWC was the only club invited to the White House for meal.

Chautauqua Women's Club
Boards, Committees
& Life Members

Janet Northrup and Jeannette Kahlenberg select pictures for the book (2008, CWC dining room)

2008 Life Member Lunch held at the Athenaeum Hotel since the group outgrew the Clubhouse.

New Life Members (2008) shown on previous page: *Patricia Beagle, Stephen Bethea III, Richard Bohn, Joann Borg, Norma Jean Bueschen, Laura Huron Collins, Emily Dean, Zetta Fradin, Ellen Freese, Sidney Holec, Nancy Langston, Linda Ludwig, Ann Lytle, Mary Pat McFarland, Bonnie Moffitt, Deloras Pemberton, Muriel Reisner, Marilyn Richey, Bonnie Rosenthal, Joan Rosenthal, Sieglinde Schwinge, Margaret Steere, Sharon Stewart, Caryl Vander Molen, Jo-An Webb and Avivah Wittenberg-Cox*

The Chautauqua Women's Club Board in 2008

Board of Directors *(alphabetical): Lynne Ballard, Margaret Bethea, Cathy Bonner, Ann T. Childs, Anita Ferguson, Ann Fletcher, Dianne Foglesong, Carole S. Glowe, Pearl K. Grosjean, Anita Holec, Diane L. Hussey, Jeannette Kahlenberg, Joan Keogh, Betty Lyons, Mary Ann McCabe, Beverley Meer, Judy Oliver, Barbara Painkin, Rita E. Paul, Rita C. Redfern, Carole Reiss, Josette Rolley, Patricia Rowe, Betty Siegel, Edie Sklar, Gwynneth Tigner, Angela Twist, Barbara E. Vackar (President), Lindsay Weidner, Margaret Worden, Grace Ferguson Zarou.*

Officers in 2008

President: Barbara Ellison Vackar (Texas),
Vice Presidents: Lynne Ballard (North Carolina), Anita Ferguson (Florida), Dianne Foglesong (Indiana), Mary Ann McCabe (New York), Angela Twist (New York)
Recording Secretary: Beverley Meer (Florida)
Corresponding Secretary: Patricia Rowe (Florida)
Registrar: Jeannette Kahlenberg (Washington)
Chaplain: Ann Childs (Connecticut)

Endowment Trustees in 2008:
Program Endowment Trustees:
Joan Keogh, Jane Lahey, Mary Ann McCabe, Dianne Foglesong
Property Endowment Trustees:
Sylvia Faust, Carole Glowe, Betty Keane, Gerry McElree,
Dianne Martin, Alyce Milks
Scholarship Endowment Trustees:
M. J. Albert, Anita Ferguson, Marjorie Kemper, Judy Oliver, Angela Twist

Associate Board of Directors 2008:
M.J. Albert, Elaine Arciszewski, Gail Gamble, Cheryl Gorelick, Patricia Hirt, Barbara Hois, Darlene Huron, Marjorie Kemper, Jane Lahey, Paula Mason, Shirley Raymond, Molly Rinehart, Susan Scott, Ann H. Sullivan, *not pictured*, Kuniko Washio

Membership photo taken 2008 courtesy of Roger Coda

**Membership of the Chautauqua Women's Club in 2008 included 729 people.
Participants shown in the 2008 group photo include the following and others:**

Meredith Andrews, Rita Argen Auerbach, Lynne Ballard, Connie Barton, LaDonna Bates, Margaret Bethea, Stephen Bethea, Charlene Bissell, Nancy Bohn, Cathy Bonner, Suzanne Brandon, Lorynne Cahn, Charles Christian, Dottie Clark, Mary Cochran, Judith Cornell, Amelia Dean, Emily Dean, Steve Dean, Amy Divijak, Anita Ferguson, Ann Fletcher, Robert Fletcher, Dianne Foglesong, Zetta Fredin, Gail Gamble, Margaret Garfield, Carole Glowe, Cheryl Gorelick, Kenneth Gorelick, Carole Griffiths, Elisabeth Groninger, Pearl Grosjean, Barbara Hois, Anita Holec, Sidney Holec, Darlene Huron, James Huron, Laura Huron Collins, Diane Hussey, Jeannette Kahlenberg, Jackie Katz, Ann Keck, Muriel Keehn, Marjorie Kemper, Joan Keogh, Jane Lahey, Susan Laubach, Eileen Leinwand, Kaye Lindauer, Dick Luehrs, Susan Luehrs, Betty Lyons, Betsy Martin, Will Martin, John McCabe, Liz McCabe, Mary Ann McCabe, Mary Pat McFarland, Anne McIntosh, Mary Jo McVicker, Beverly Meer, Richard Meer, Tibb Middleton, Alyce Milks, Chris Milks, Sandra Miller, Iris November, Francie Oliver, Judy Oliver, Patricia Panebianco, Rita Paul, Mary Jane Pringle, Rita Redfern, Carole Reeder, Carole Reiss, Josette Rolley, Gladys Ross, Maureen Rovegno, Patricia Rowe, Carol Rufener, Susan Scott, Sheldon Seligsohn, Mary Jane Shank, Betsy Siegel, Edie Sklar, Stephanie Smith, LaVada Steed, Sharon Lee Stewart, Ann Sullivan, Marlene Thibault, Angela Twist, Joseph Twist, Barbara Vackar, Ann Walsh, Kuniko Washio, Lindsay Weidner, Joan Wilson, Lou Wineman, Ann Winkelstein, Margaret Worden, and Andrea Zarou.

THE 2007 SCHOLARSHIP COMMITTEE

SEATED: Lucille Piper (FL), Marjorie Kemper (PA)* Anita Ferguson, (FL)*
ROW 1: Juanita Jackson (NY), Lorynne Cahn (FL), Sylvia Miller (WI), Ann Winklestein (PA), Mary Jane Shank (NY), Hope Alcorn (PA), Kuniko Washio (FL), Carole Reiss (FL)
ROW 2: Angela Twist (NY), Jean Nickerson (FL), Edie Teibel (NY), Marshall Nelson, Elaine Arciszewski (NJ)
ROW 3: Marjorie Sterritte (FL), Anne Prezio (FL), Ruth Mohney (NY)
ROW 4: Jean Wilson (PA), Susan Wood (FL), Richard Kemper (far back) (PA), Ann Weber (PA), Judy Bachleitner (NY), Barbara Hois (PA)

Marjorie Kemper and Anita Ferguson have served as Chair of Scholarship

Taking Care of the Clubhouse for Eighty Years, Then and Now

BUILDING FUND COMMITTEE COMMITTEE
1929

Mrs. Frank Warren Smith	(NJ)
Mrs. Robert E. Anderson	(PA)
Mrs. R. W. Argue	(KS)
Miss Gertrude Blodgett	(NY)
Mrs. Charles Bonner	(TX)
Mrs. J. G. Cohoe	(MS)
Mrs. Lawrence Cornell	(NY)
Mrs. Mary Ducorron	(MO)
Miss Mary O. Duncan	(PA)
Mrs. Davis Edwards	(IL)
Mrs. John Gillespie	(PA)
Miss Anne Grey	(D.C.)
Mrs. Ross Hood	(PA)
Miss Flora Jones	(PA)
Miss Mabel Keeler	(NY)
Mrs. Waldine Kopperl	(TX)
Mrs. J. C. Lewis	(PA)
Mrs. R. B. Logan	(TN)
Mrs. Charles Menet	(NJ)
Mrs. Lillian G. Smith	(FL)

BUILDING COMMITTEE
1929

Mrs. R.W. Argue	(KS)
Mrs. Charles T. Bonner	(TX)
Miss Gertrude Blodgett	(NY
Mrs. Lillian G. Smith	(FL)

SPECIAL ASSISTANTS TO THE BUILDING FUND COMMITTEE

1929

Mrs. S. M. Palmer	(PA)
Mrs. George W. Plummer	(IL)
Mrs. W. H. Alexander	(PA)
Mrs. George Thatcher	(KS)

HOUSE ENDOWMENT COMMITTEE
2009

Kathy Bruhn	(IL)
Patricia Dietly	(PA)
Aggie Fausnaugh	(OH)
Sylvia Faust	(NY)
Carole Glowe	(OH)
Carole Griffiths	(OH)
Patricia Hirt	(AZ)
Joan Keogh	(FL)
Bette Keane	(MA)
Jane Lahey	(IL)
Dianne Martin	(OH)
Gerry McElree	(PA)
Alyce Milks	(FL)
Rita Paul	(FL)
Sue Ann Power	(CA)
Molly Rinehart	(FL)
Josette Rolley	(IN)
Pat Rowe	(FL)
Helen Snyder	(NY)
Marian Stranburg	(FL)

HOUSE COMMITTEE
2009

CO-CHAIRS for OPERATIONS
Darlene Huron and Josette Rolley

Margaret Bethea	(GA)
Dick Meer	(FL)
Dottie Clark	(OH)
Diane Hussey	(TN)
Rita Redfern	(FL)

2009 HOUSE SUBCOMMITTEES:

ARCHITECTURE AND INTERIOR DESIGN

Ann Fletcher, Chair	(FL)
Lindsay Weidner	(FL)
Dottie Clark	(OH)
Cheryl Gorelick	(DC)

LANDSCAPING

Betsy Martin	(TX)

Year 2009 Board of Directors

President and Board Members
Barbara Ellison Vackar, Pres.

Cathy Bonner, Anita Ferguson, Ann Fletcher, Pearl Grosjean, Anita Holec, Betty Lyons, Barbara Painkin, Ann Sullivan, Patricia Rowe

Edie Sklar, Dianne Foglesong, Jeannette Kahlenberg, Joan Keogh, Beverley Meer, Betty Siegel, Betsy Martin, Angela Twist, Lindsay Weidner

Diane Hussey, Margaret Bethea, Gwynneth Tigner, Rita Redfern, Josette Rolley, Pat Hirt, Darlene Huron, Virginia DiPucci, Barbara Hois, Paula Mason

Associate Board 2009

Elaine Arciszewski, Lynne Ballard, Ann Childs, Laura Collins, Gail Gamble, Cheryl Gorelick, Marjorie Kemper, Jane Lahey, Mary Ann McCabe, Mary Pat McFarland, Sandy Miller, Janet Northrup, Judy Oliver, Carole Reiss, Kuniko Washio

Vice Presidents
Dianne Foglesong, Anita Holec, Darlene Huron, Angela Twist, Edie Sklar

Recording Secretary
Beverley Meer

Corresponding Secretary
Patricia Rowe

Treasurer
Gwynneth Tigner

Registrar
Jeannette Kahlenberg

Nominating
Edie Sklar, Barbara Hois, Mary Ann McCabe

Chaplain
Pearl Grosjean

Endowment Trustees
Program: Dianne Foglesong Joan Keogh, Jane Lahey, Mary Ann McCabe
Property: Sylvia Faust, Betty Keane, Dianne Martin, Alyce Milks, Gerry McElree, Patricia Rowe
Scholarship: Anita Ferguson, M. J. Albert, Judy Oliver, Marjorie Kemper, Angela Twist

Publicity
Virginia DiPucci

A Changing Organization

The Chautauqua Women's Club has been supporting the Institution's programs for 120 years, while also providing members with the opportunity to experience new ideas and develop lasting friendships. The welcoming Clubhouse offers a foundation for women and men, people of different ages and varying interests and talents. Members take pride in supporting the philanthropic efforts that bring hundreds of enthusiastic scholarship students to Chautauqua. The Club is not the same as it was in 1889, even though programs stimulate and inform as they did decades ago. At the beginning the organization was top-down, when few women were educated and consequently looked to the CWC Presidents for informative programs. In addition to the popular cooking classes, programs in 1890 also included these lectures: "Foundation Stones of Character"; First Principles of Dress"; "Economy and Waste"; "Philosophy of Housekeeping"; "How to Awaken and Sustain a Wider Interest in Missions"; "Prevention of Intemperance"; and "Mistakes in Education." Club members in 2009 come from more diverse backgrounds and have had educational opportunities that were unavailable to the participants in 1889. In 2008 the CWC sponsored forty-six recitals by students and their instructors and thirteen lectures through the Contemporary Issues Forum. In contrast to 1889, lectures in 2008 included: "How Blogs and Polls Affect Elections"; "Surveying the Landscape of Healthcare Reform"; "Autism: Stories from a Health Care Crisis"; "Developing Leaders for the Twenty-first Century"; "Maintaining Amateur Status in Intercollegiate Athletics"; "What Is Compassionate Pain Care in the 21st Century?" and "Social Action to End Domestic Violence." Members often look for a committee where they can serve, meet others, learn and give back to the community in the time they have at Chautauqua. Club officers must understand the various endowment committees, service opportunities and other activities and then endeavor to harmonize the work of different groups.

The meeting place itself has been a focus since women first met at Chautauqua in 1874. The present Clubhouse is a desirable facility in a picturesque setting, but the leaders face the problem of maintaining an eighty-year-old building that is occupied for only nine weeks during the Season and is in need of modernization. Through volunteerism, dedication, innovations and group efforts, no doubt the leadership will solve the current problems and continue to offer outstanding educational opportunities to the members and Chautauqua community. The 2009 Executive Board invites everyone who visits Chautauqua to stop by the Women's Club, participate in Club activities, consider membership and experience this historic inclusive organization.

Mary Lou Goodman, Mary Jane Shank, Pat Stine, Tibb Middleton beside the Club entrance and Chautauqua Lake

Lucille Piper at "Artists at the Market Crafters"

CONTEMPORARY ISSUES SERIES
Leadership Continues at the CWC

For over two decades the CWC scheduled approximately seventeen speakers each "Season" (two each week) who discussed issues that often differed from the theme week planned by Chautauqua Institution. These lectures gave audiences insight on another "topic of interest," many of which are mentioned in this book. Lectures varied from spousal abuse to stem cell research while speakers included a female astronaut, the Director of the World Food Bank, judges, magazine editors, doctors, professors and business leaders. Starting in 2009, one Contemporary Issues lecture will be scheduled each Saturday afternoon. Instead of a second mid-week lecture, the Women's Club, together with Chautauqua Institution, will host a "dialogue" with one of the Institution's Amphitheater lecturers. This new program is designed to give audience members a chance to have an interchange of ideas on a topic with one of the prominent Amphitheater speakers.

In 2006 the Women's Club was proud to add a new "named lecture" to the Contemporary Issues Series through the Brown-Giffin Endowment. The excitement and quality of this lecture has enhanced the Chautauqua program and is evidence of the support the CWC gives the Institution. The Women's Club continues to influence national movements and interests by providing a forum for 21st Century ideas, discussion groups and "net-working" opportunities.

Women were not encouraged to speak at the Assembly in 1874, but the speaker of 2008's Brown-Giffin lecture was the nationally recognized female journalist/newscaster, Jane Pauley. Whereas the Suffragists rallied for "The Vote", the 2007 Brown-Giffin speaker interpreted the law and was the first female U.S. Supreme Court Justice. While most Nineteenth Century Chautauqua women were "home makers" interested in Ewing's "cooking and castle building," women in 2009 might join a professional networking group *and* develop other interests, including (perhaps) cooking and/or a castle building. The current Club President, for example, ran a catering business, worked on the Equal Rights legislation, advocated for consumer credit counseling for families and participated in political leadership. Now women have choices of careers in business, education, law, the Arts and medicine and greater financial independence as a result of education, legislation and societal changes. In their own way, today's Chautauqua women are founding women with the choices and accomplishments they make and by their influence on others. They are the role models for younger women (and younger men) today and for those of the future. Certainly the teenaged women who attended the conversation with Justice O'Connor at the CWC will not forget the ideas from that mentoring opportunity.

One popular presenter at the Contemporary Issues Forum is Dr. Martha Reitman, who has spoken frequently on health issues such as stem cell uses. Another well-received speaker at the Forum is Professor David Kozak, who has participated for over twenty years. Dr. Kozak, Director of Public Policy at Gannon College in Erie, also was a visiting professor at West Point Military Academy. His lectures always give a cogent analysis of national politics. These speakers and others show the educational opportunity the CWC provides the Chautauqua community today.

Dianne Foglesong, Mary Ann McCabe,
Justice Sandra Day O'Connor, Barbara Vackar

The twenty Presidents of the Chautauqua Women's Club (1889-2009) and other members held leadership roles in the following organizations or programs. The Women's Club truly is an organization of leaders and learners that affected and continues to affect the Chautauqua Institution, regional, state, national and international groups.

AAUW American Association of University Women
      (General Director and various leadership positions)
Advisory Committee on the Arts, John F. Kennedy administration
American Cancer Society (Leader of volunteers)
Brown-Giffin Lecture (Chautauqua program addition)
Chautauqua Board of Trustees
Chautauqua Literary and Scientific Circle (Pres. of Pioneer Class)
Chautauqua Poetry Contest and various writing programs, 1931-2006
Chautauqua Recreational Center (Director)
Chautauqua Symphony Orchestra (Guarantors)
(Continued on next page)

Church World Service-Kosovo Relief Project
Contemporary Issues Lectures (CWC program)
Daughters of the American Revolution
Equal Rights Amendment
Evanston College for Ladies-founder (forerunner of Northwestern Female College) Dean
Fifty-Five Plus Program at Chautauqua Institution (Creator and Director)
General Federation of Women's Clubs (Nat. Pres. and State Presidents)
Girl Scouts of America (National Director)
Hospital Volunteer Interpreter Program (founder) Rochester, NY
International Alliance of Women for Suffrage and Equal Citizenship
League of Nations (supporter/reporter of events to U.S. newspapers)
Metropolitan Opera Company ("Curtain Talks" commentator)
National Board of Foreign Missions for the Presbyterian Church
National Committee on the Cause and Cure of War 1936-1941 (Chair)
National Council of Presbyterian Women (Executive Committee)
National Federation of Music Clubs (Pres.)
National League of Woman's Service (1918)
National League of Women Voters (Director of International Relations)
National Service School (branch at Chautauqua/Commandant)
National Woman's Suffrage Association (NWSA)
New York State General Federation of Women's Clubs
Pan Pacific Women's Association
Regent, State of Pennsylvania
Purdue University, Director of the Department of Domestic Economy
Scholarship Program awards to artists, musicians, and dancers at Chautauqua Institution
The Women's Christian Temperance Union (President)
Textbook of Texas History (author of first history textbook used in Texas)
U.N.E.S.C.O. (United States conference delegate) Pres. Richard Nixon administration
University/college teaching (Vassar, Pennsylvania State University and others)
Woman's Self-Care Center in Jamestown (support); contributor to the following regional
groups: Chautauqua Lake Association; Chautauqua Watershed Conservancy; Bell Tower
Scholarship; the Chautauqua Foundation; Chautauqua Fire Department

Milestones
◆ of the ◆
Chautauqua Women's Club

1874- Fair Point holds an Assembly led by Lewis Miller and John Heyl Vincent; three women speak at the Assembly platform

1874- Women meet separately at Chautauqua, a Victorian custom for men and women to hold separate functions

1876- Frances Willard addresses the Assembly on Temperance

1882- Susan B. Anthony speaks at Chautauqua on Women's Suffrage

1889- The Women's Club is founded as an official organization

1906- The CWC dues raised to 50 cents, partially to fund summer school scholarships

1901- The CWC produces its first Yearbook

1917- 1918 Women acquire the first Clubhouse on Janes and South Lake

1920- The First Clubhouse is paid for in full

1920's- Jeanette Bestor hosts the CWC Golden Belles for a tea at the President's house

1922- The CWC hosts the convention of the General Federation of Women's Clubs

1929- The CWC builds a permanent Clubhouse and opens on July 3, 1929

1931- A Poetry Contest is held with awards made through the CWC

1935- 1700 members of the CWC are invited to the White House. Eleanor Roosevelt offers lunch to the group; 903 CWC members went to Washington

1936- John D. Rockefeller Jr. writes check to the Chautauqua Women's Club for $37,000, later presented at Old First Night to write off CI (Depression) debt

1945- Junior Women's Group is started at the CWC with programs and service options

1947- The Club offers scholarships to promising music students $300 is awarded

1947- The CWC hosts the National Federation of Music Clubs

1948- Men are included as associate members

1949- The CWC celebrates sixty years; hobby show with 60 vendors is held

1950- Scholarships are raised to $1000

1960's- A new charter is created with a permanent Certificate of Incorporation for NY

1967- The "Happy to Meet You" event starts at the beginning of the Season

1969- The Property Endowment Fund is established

1970's- The Writing Symposia begins

1970's- The Property Endowment Fund reaches $95,000

1974- E. Dorothy Dann Bullock writes "Chautauqua Women's Club: Eighty-Five Years"

1976- The CWC holds its first "Berry Fest", later known as the Strawberry Festival

1979- The Clubhouse celebrates fifty years of service

1979- E. Dorothy Dann Bullock writes "Fifty Years of Service"

1986- The Property Endowment is established

1986- The CWC starts the Antique Show

1986- Kodak travelogues are added

1987- The CWC celebrates member Helen Jacobs for service and 60 years as a member

1988- The CWC holds a reception for U. S. Supreme Court Justice Sandra Day O'Connor

1989- Alfreda Irwin writes "Chautauqua Women's Club History 1889-1999"
1990-1991- The Annual scholarships are raised to $16,100 and then $17,200
1992- The Contemporary Issues Forum begins
1992- CWC Program Endowment Fund begins
1998- The Scholarship Endowment is established
1999-125th Anniversary of CI; the Women's Club contributes items to the time capsule
2001- 02 Website is developed
2004- 75th Anniversary of the Clubhouse is celebrated
2005- Club logo was created by Tibb Middleton
2005- $45,175 is given to the Chautauqua Fund through efforts of fund-raisers and
        contributors
2006- The Steinway piano is sent to Astoria, Queens for renovation
2006- Beverly Dame Esch retires; Scholarship Committee donates over $83,000
2006- Koffee Klub group starts; discuss topics of interest
2006- The Brown-Giffin family endows a lecture fund
2007- The Steinway piano returns to the House and Beverly Dame Esch is honored
2007- The roof is replaced; a front column is renovated
2007- Sandra Day O'Connor speaks in the Amphitheater under auspices of the CWC
        Contemporary Issues Forum and Chautauqua Institution
2007- Justice O'Connor meets with young women in the CWC
2008- The CWC donates over $100,750 in scholarships
2008- New landscaping in front of house is created, The Anita Garden
2008- Jane Pauley speaks at the Club; Brown-Giffin lecture: "Talking About Mental
        Illness"
2008- A group photo is taken of the whole CWC
2008- Plans are made for major house upgrades and funding campaigns
2009- Contemporary Issues Dialogues begin as a cooperative effort between the
        Chautauqua Women's Club and Chautauqua Institution, held weekly. The
        Dialogues offer an opportunity for interaction with an Amphitheater speaker
2009- Janet Northrup writes *Founding Women*: *Inspiration and Impact on Chautauqua
        and the Nation*, a history of 135 years at CI
2009- A new patio at the CWC is created from "Friendship Bricks"
2009- Author Gail Sheehy (Brown-Giffin Lecture) speaks on "Caregiving"
2009- Group networking Chautauqua professional women is developed
2009- The CWC celebrates 120 years as an official organization, 1889 to 2009

As the Chautauqua Women's Club turns 120 years old in 2009, abundant opportunities are offered during the nine week Chautauqua Season. The Women's Club has scheduled forty-five programs, eighteen board and committee meetings, 119 fund raisers (including 48 recitals), nine group events such as the Life Member Lunch, three Teen Nights, one Teen Recital Night, seventeen bridge classes and eighteen Mah Jongg sessions. The historic house continues to inspire and impact people of different interests and ages and is a prominent educational force through the Contemporary Issues Forum and the Brown-Giffin lectures.

A Life Member Lunch when they were held at the Women's Club
Marianne Karslake, Josette Rolley, Judy Cornell, Carole Reiss, Mary Ann McCabe

"Mark & Rita Party" 2008
Seated: Mary Jane Shank. Standing (l. to r.) Ginny Putnam, Virginia DiPucci, Rita
Auerbach, Barbara Vackar, Dottie Clark, Susan Luehrs, Audre Bunis, Renee Schecter, Cathy
Bonner. Top Row: Tibb Middleton

LIFE MEMBERS OF THE CHAUTAUQUA WOMEN'S CLUB 2009

Life Membership pins

Adams, Sarah, FL; Adler, Elaine, NJ; Albert, M.J., NY; Alexander, Joan B., NY; Alexander, Susan, PA; Altschuler, Mark, NJ; Anderson, Barbara, MD; Anderson, Peggy, AZ; Andrews, Beth, MN; Andrews, Meredith, NY; Antemann, Kristin Doebler, SC; Anthony, Paul, DC; Apfel, Kenneth, MD; Arciszewski, Elaine, NJ; Arena, Kristine, MA; Arnn, Deborah L., FL; Arnold, Margaret L., ; Aron, Eleanor R., OH; Artico, Susan, NY; Auerbach, Rita Argen, NY; Babcock, James, NY; Babcock, Sherri, NY; Bagley, Vicki, FL; Ballard, Lynne E., NC; Barber, Linda, NY; Bargar, Kristen E., NY; Barrett-Orr, Barbara, VA; Barton, Connie, CA; Bates, LaDonna G., PA; Bates, William, PA; Beagle, Patricia S., NY; Bean, Shirley, NY; Bechtolt, Nancy, AZ; Becker, Jane, NY; Becker, Tom, NY; Bedrosian, Emogene, NY; Bellowe, Jill, CA; Berg, Karen, FL; Bethea, Dr. Stephen, GA; Bethea, Margaret D., GA; Bissell, Caroline VanKirk, AZ; Bohn, Nancy, NJ; Bohn, Richard, NJ; Bonner, Cathy, TX; Bonsignore, Susan, NY; Borg, JoAnn, CA; Borowsky, Martha J., PA; Boucher, Jeannette, FL; Bower, Diana, CA; Bower, Loretta E., OH; Boyd, Bonita, NY; Bozic, Rebecca, PA; Bradford, Ellis, NC; Brady, Barbara, GA; Branch, Amy, NY; Branch, Barbara, NC; Branch, Paul M., NY; Branch-Prince, Laurie, NY; Brandon, Suzanne, AZ; Bratton, Wanita, NY; Brenner, Loretta J., MD; Brewer, Nancy, CA; Broad, Ecky, OH; Brooks, Marva, GA; Brown, Mary, FL; Brown, Max, FL; Brown, Patricia Mahoney, NY; Bruhn, Kathleen, IL; Buerk, Jill Raisen, NY; Bueschen, Norma Jean, GA; Bunis, Audre, NY; Burden, Anne, FL; Burdman, Babette, AZ; Burgwardt, Clarice H., NY; Burr, Kristi Schmitt, OH; Bush, Kathleen, MD; Buxbaum, Margery, TN; Byrd, Bonnie P., FL; Cahn, Lorynne, FL; Campbell, Rev. Dr. Joan Brown, OH; Campen, Jacqueline P., FL; Carlisle, Bert, OH; Carlisle, Marian, state unknown; Cawein, Paul, NY; Chaffee, Charlotte, PA; Chaverin, Lee, FL; Chimente, James J., NC; Christian, Charles, FL; Ciancio, Marilyn, NY; Citron, Philip, NY; Clark, Dorothy, FL; Clark, Dottie, FL; Clark, Jerine W., OH; Clarke, Mrs. Joseph C., state unknown; Clementi, Debi, FL; Clendenning, Elizabeth, NH; Cline, Dorothy, FL; Clouse, Joan Reed, NY; Cochran, Mary Reed, PA; Coffman, Jane, VA; Cole, Ruth Gerrard, OH; Coleman, Nancy Strong, PA; Conarro, Mary E., PA; Conway, Jeanne, OH; Corcoran, Rosemary E., OH; Cornell, Chloe, FL; Cornell, Helen, MD; Cornell, Judith Ann, FL; Corry, Emily McKnight, NY; Court, Georgia, OH; Cowles, Handy, NY; Cox, Virginia, VA; Cram, Mary Frances, NJ; Crowder, Karen, TX; Cullen, Linda, FL; Curatolo, Kathleen, FL; Daley, Mary Elizabeth, VA; Damon, Laura, NY; Daniels, Myra Janco, FL; Dasent, Carlton, MA; Davis, Nina, TX; Dean, Amelia, PA; Dean, Emily, PA; Dean, Steve, PA; Deblinger, JoAnn, NY; DeMott, Elmore, AL; Denton, Anna F., NY; Denton, S. Melissa, MI; DeVillars, John Pierre, MA; Diggs, Dr. Nancy, OH; DiPucci, Virginia, PA; Divijak, Amy, AZ; Duhme, Carol M., MO; Eddie, Lorraine, Canada; Eddins, Essie A., NY; Eden, Jack, MD; Edgington, Helen, NY; Edwards, Tracy, CA; Ehrenreich, Rivona, NY; Einstein, Laura G., CT; Eisenhower, David, PA; Eisenhower, Julie Nixon, PA; Esch, Beverly Dame, NY; Evans, Phyllis, ; Evans, Renee, OH; Everett, Edith B., NY; Fausnaugh, Agnes, OH; Faust, Sylvia, NY; Fay, Celia, PA; Fechter, George, PA; Ferguson, Anita, FL; Ferguson-Zarou, Grace, NC; First, Deborah, NY; Fleck, Shelagh, Canada; Fleming, Charlotte, TN; Fletcher, Ann, FL; Fletcher,

Robert K., FL; Flickinger, Dr. Bonnie, NY; Foglesong, Dianne, IN; Fountain, Joanna, ; Fowler, Charlotte, OH; Fradin, Zetta, FL; Freese, Ellen M, NY; Freese, Norma F., NY; Fromson, Suzanne, FL; Fugo, Denise Marie, OH; Furman, Kathryn M., FL; Galloway, Lois T., NY; Gamble, Gail, FL; Garfield, Margaret, SC; Garza, Jocelyn Rolley, TX; Gelfand, Michael J., FL; Gentry, Jeannie, AZ; Georgescu, Barbara, NY; Gerhold, Mary E., CA; Gibson, Ann Lee, MO; Gierszal, Paula, NY; Giffin, Donald, MO; Giffin, Esther Atha, MO; Gladstone, Carole E., CT; Glasgow, Kim, CA; Glowe, Carole S., OH; Golay, Clara W., NC; Goldberg, Patricia C., TX; Goldfarb, Toni, NJ; Goldman, Judy, MO; Goldman, Patricia, DC; Goodman, Marylou, OH; Gootnick, Margery F., NY; Gordon, Sondra, NJ; Gorelick, Cheryl, DC; Gorelick, Dr. Kenneth P., DC; Greb, Karen B., PA; Greenhouse, Donald, NY; Greenhouse, Kathleen, NY; Gregory, Judith, NC; Griewahn, Nancy J., FL; Griewahn, Pamela, PA; Griewahn/Okita, Jessamine, VA; Griffiths, Carole, OH; Groninger, Elisabeth, VA; Grosjean, Pearl K., OH; Gross, Jane, NY; Grover, Candy, OH; Handley, Mary F., NY; Hanlon, Denise, NY; Hansen, Jane, PA; Hanson, Carol, OH; Hanson, Judy, NY; Hauck, Terrie Vaile, VA; Haupt, Eleanor McKnight, PA; Hauser, Jane, NC; Hawkes, Lesley, United Kingdom; Hawthorne, Jane, OH; Hegarty, Christopher, state unknown; Hendrickson, Dorothy Dow, KY; Hennessa, Gail, VA; Herron, Marilyn, FL; Hess, Diane R., SC; Hicks, Carolyn, FL; Highberger, Joanne S., PA; Hilbinger, Terriann, PA; Hill, Dorothy Sample, PA; Hirsh, Carol Nobel, NY; Hirt, Patricia, AZ; Hois, Barbara, PA; Holden, Arlene, OH; Holec, Anita V., FL; Holec, Dr. Sidney, FL; Hootnick, Sally, NY; Howell, Judith E., FL; Huron, Darlene, FL; Huron, James, FL; Huron Collins, Laura, OH; Hussey, Diane L., TN; Hutton, Karol, state unknown; Ingram, Joan Bailey, United Kingdom; Irion, Mary Jean, PA; Jackson, Juanita Wallace, NY; Jacob, Barbara, FL; Jacobs, Joan, PA; Jacoby, Sara B., FL; Jamison, Eleanor S., NC; Johnson, Elinor V., OH; Jones, Barbara C., TX; Jones, Linda Winters, VT; Jones, Mildred Gordon, GA; Jones, Mrs. B.G., NC; Kahlenberg, Jeannette, WA; Kammerman, Theresa, OH; Kantor, Kim Ciccarelli, FL; Karslake, Marianne, PA; Karslake, Richard, PA; Keating, Caroline, NY; Keck, Ann T., NY; Keogh, Joan, FL; Keyser, Barbara, TX; Khosh, Mary, FL; Kim, Patricia A., NY; Kirstein, Roslyn, NY; Klier, Mary McMahon, FL; Kling, Mrs. David, ; Klingensmith, Patricia, PA; Kobacker, Cathe Chapin, OH; Krall, Nancy, NY; Kriska, Chloe Ann, OH; Krueger, Linda, TX; Kuhn, Marguerite S., ; Kunze, Mary M., WI; Kyler, Nancy, VA; Lahey, Jane, IL; Lamprecht, Marjorie, ; Langsam, Renee, FL; Langston, Nancy, PA; Lasky, Sylvia P., NY; Lazroe, Althea Ann Darner, NY; Lee, Cherylynne, CA; Lefever, Margaret Tate, PA; Lehman, Ann, PA; Leinwand, Eileen, TN; Leonard, Nathalie, ; Levine, Nancy, CT; Levine, Samson, CT; Lewis, Miriam W., NY; Lichtman, Jacqueline, VA; Lindauer, Kaye, NY; Livingstone, Pearl, OH; Lloyd, Amy, MA; Lollis, Betty, KY; Longtain, Melinda, TX; Ludwig, Linda, OH; Luehrs, Margaret, FL; Luehrs, Susan, FL; Luik, Janet, Canada; Lutton, Bonnie G. Devries, IL; Lyons, Betty, PA; Lytle, Ann, PA; Machleder, Elaine, NY; MacKenzie, Flora, VA; MacKenzie, Ross, VA; Maloney, Dorothea A., OH; Markman, Tomi, state unknown; Markowski, Carolyn, FL; Markowski, Jerome, FL; Marter, Lenore, OH; Martin, Betsy, TX; Martin, Chris, PA; Martin, Dianne K., OH; Martin, Susan, PA; Martin, Will P., TX; Mason, Paula, MD; McBrier, Blossom, PA; McCabe, Elizabeth, NY; McCabe, Mary Ann, NY; McCabe, Rosemarie Hidalgo, VA; McClure, Ann, CA; McConnon, Henry K. (Van), NY; McElree, Dr. Frank E., PA; McElree, Gerry, PA; McFate, Mary, FL; McIntosh, Anne Capper, Australia; McKalip, Adele, ; McKee, Lisa Gierszal, NY; McKee, Susan, CO; McKenzie, Lydia Chaverin, FL; McKibbin, Roberta, NY; McReynolds, Erna, NY; McVay, Hella, NJ; McVay, Scott, NJ; McVicker, Mary Jo, state unknown; Meer, Beverley, FL; Milks, Alyce, FL; Milks, Chris, OH; Milks, Dr. Donald E., FL; Miller, Barbara B., TX; Miller, Sandra, PA; Moffitt, Bonnie, RI; Mohney, Ruth W., NY; Monceaux, Francoise, DC; Moore, Jane Ross, OH; Moore McGee, Rebecca, WA; Morgan, Tom, NY; Murphy, Charlotte, NY; Muse, Karen A., FL; Newhall, Karen M., FL; Newton, Roberta, PA; Norris, Marjorie, NY; Northrup, Janet, NY; Norton, Florence, NY; November, Iris, OH; O'Brien, Heather, OH; Ocel, Janet, PA; O'Connor (RET), Justice Sandra Day, DC; Oliver, Francie, TX; Oliver, Hale, PA; Oliver, Judy, PA; Oliver, Sharon, NY; Painkin, Barbara, FL; Panebianco, Patricia Jean, AZ; Pankow, Arthur E., NY; Paul, Rita E., FL; Pemberton, Deloras, KS; Pembridge, Rosalie H., SC; Periard, Carol, IL; Perlis, Linda S., MD; Peters, Sarah+C436 Myers, VA; Peterson, Cynthia Howard, NY; Prezio, Anne T., FL; Pringle, Mary Jane, AZ; Pugh, Mary Alice, FL; Putnam, Ginny,

NY; Raab, Pat Tinker, FL; Rappole, Jennifer, MA; Raymond, Shirley L., NY; Read, Gwen Shell, FL; Reading, Miriam, WI; Redfern, Rita C., PA; Reeder, Carole, SC; Reeder, Robert, SC; Reid, Margaret Dunbar, ; Reimann, Lee B., MI; Reisner, Muriel C., FL; Reiss, Carole, FL; Reiss, Clemens, FL; Reitman, Dr. Martha, CA; Reitman, Karen, CA; Reitman, Laura, CA; Remick, Emma L, ME; Richey, Marilyn, FL; Rieck, Debra, PA; Rieser, Susie, IL; Rinehart, Molly, FL; Ritacco, Joanne, DC; Robb, Jean F., PA; Robins, Eunice, AZ; Robinson, Ann, FL; Robinson, Emilie W., MD; Rockwell, Helen S., PA; Roederer, Charlotte, NY; Rolley, Cheryl, IN; Rolley, Josette A., IN; Rolley, Larissa, IL; Rose, Jane G., NY; Rosenthal, Bonnie, FL; Rosenthal, Joan, NY; Rousseau, Meredith C., PA; Rovegno, Maureen A., NY; Rowe, Patricia H., FL; Ruis, Pamela Griewahn, OH; Russell, Donna M., SC; Sammarco, Ruthann, OH; Sanders, Dale, FL; Sauser, Virginia, NJ; Schaffer, Donna, FL; Schaus, Joanne, OH; Schecter, Renee, OH; Schmitt, Eleanor D., OH; Schott, Mildred I., PA; Schrader, Nancy, NJ; Schuckers, Barbara A., NY; Schuder, Jean D., NY; Schultz, Phyllis, NC; Schwinge, Sieglinde "Sigi", NY; Scott, Susan B., FL; Sedelmyer, Kerry Rovegno, PA; Selden, Nikki, OH; Selkregg, Jean, PA; Shafer, Maura, WI; Shames, Ben, FL; Shames, Enid, FL; Shank, Mary Jane, NY; Sheng, Shao Fang, WV; Siegel, Betty, FL; Sklar, Edie, CA; Small, Dorothy J., NY; Smith, Joan A., NY; Smith, Ted, TX; Smolinski, Edie, VA; Snyder, Paula, ; Speers-Sivak, Joyce, FL; Spink, Prudence, OH; Spraragen, Nancy, FL; Stage, Alyson Cook, WA; Steed, LaVada, TX; Steere, , MA; Stewart, Sharon, AL; Stine, Patricia, MD; Stinson, Lynn Heiserling, MI; Stolberg, Mary Howard, MI; Stranburg, Marian C., FL; Strother, George, MD; Strother, Marianne, MD; Sullivan, Ann H., NY; Taber, Nancy, FL; Talpas, Nanci, FL; Tate, Joyce, FL; Thibault, Marlene, UT; Thurston, Jean, FL; Tigner, Gwynneth, NY; Townsend, Carol, NY; Trefts, Joan L., OH; Twist, Angela, NY; Twist, Joseph, MD; Ugoletti, Mary, PA; Ulrich-Hagner, Linda, NY; Vackar, Barbara, TX; Vander Molen, Caryl, NY; Viehe, Carol, PA; Viehe, Margaret, CA; Viehe, Richard, CA; Voboril, Melanie, AZ; Voll, Joan, Canada; Waller, Sylvia, FL; Washio, Kuniko, FL; Weaver, Frances, ; Webb, Jo-An, FL; Weidner, Lindsay, FL; Weiler, F. Mina Miller, CO; Weinberg, Hannah, NY; Weiner, Beatrice, FL; Weinstein, Claire, NJ; Weinstein, Judge Gerald, NJ; Weinstock, Ruth, ; Welch, Dr. Martha G., NY; Wendler, Ken, TX; Westcott, Page, Canada; Westgren, Barbara, PA; Westwater, Lisa M., OH; White, Anne D., state unknown; Wightman, Yvonne L., state unknown; Wiley, Phyllis, OH; Wilhelm, Donna, FL; Willen, Sybil, OH; Williams, Nina T., OH; Wilmot, Phyllis Hodill, NJ; Wilson, Jean, PA; Wilson, Norma, FL; Wineman, Lou B., NY; Winkelstein, Ann P., PA; Wittenberg-Cox, Avivah, France; Wolf, Elizabeth H., OH; Wolinski, Jessica F., CA; Wood, Susan O., FL; Wunderlich, Joyce C., NY; Young, Marilyn, OH; Zaretsky, Deborah, NY; Zarou, Dr. Donald, NY; Zarou, Rev. Andrea, NY; Zausner, Violet, FL; Zuegel, Barbara B., NY;

Members in 2009 make their homes in 33 states, Washington D.C. and four countries

ENDNOTES

[1] E. Dorothy Dann Bullock, *Chautauqua Women's Club Chautauqua, New York, The History of Eighty-five Years 1989-1974.* Chautauqua Women's Club, 1975, 24.

[2] Bullock, *Eighty-five Years,* 24.

[3] Bullock, E. Dorothy Dann, *Chautauqua Women's Club: Fifty Years Service of the Club House,* July 27, 1979, *1.*

[4] Pauline Fancher, *Chautauqua: Its Architecture and People* (Miami: Banyan Books, 1978) 72.

[5] Fancher 98.

[6] Karen Crowder, personal interview, 17 Aug. 2008.

[7] Paul Leone and Mary Poshka, *Around Chautauqua Lake: Fifty Years of Photographs 1875-1925* (Westfield: Chautauqua Region Press, 1997) viii.

[8] Leone viii.

[9] Kathleen Crocker and Jane Currie, *Images of America: Chautauqua Institution* (Charleston, S.C.: Arcadia Publishing Company, 2001) 10.

[10] Jeffrey Simpson, *Chautauqua, An American Utopia* (New York: Harry N. Abrams Inc., 1999) 33.

[11] Bullock, *Eighty-five Years* 3.

[12] Bullock, *Eighty-five Years* 3.

[13] Crocker and Currie 107.

[14] WCTU official website, 2008.

[15] Alfreda Irwin, *Chautauqua Women's Club History 1889-1989,* 1-2.

[16] Bullock, *Eighty-five Years* 4.

[17] Irwin 2.

[18] Irwin 2.

[19] Irwin 3.

[20] Bullock, *Eighty-five Years* 25.

[21] Irwin 10.

[22] Irwin 8.

[23] Bullock, *Eighty-five Years* 4.

[24] Fancher 4.

[25] Bullock, *Eighty-five Years* 5.

[26] Bullock, *Eighty-five Years* 5-6.

[27] Bullock, *Eighty-five Years* 7

[28] Fancher 22.

[29] T. C. Flood, Ed. *The Chautauqua Assembly Herald,* Vol. XV 2 Aug. 1890, 1.

[30] *"The Chautauqua Assembly Herald"* 8 Aug. 1890, 4.

[31] *"The Chautauqua Assembly Herald." 26 July, 1890, 4.*

[32] Alice Ross, "The Mysterious Disappearance of Lard," *Hearth to Hearth,* Feb. 2002.

[33] Fancher 7.

[34] Bullock, *Eighty-five Years* 7.

[35] Bullock, *Eighty-five Years,* 7-8.

[36] Bullock, *Eighty-five Years,* 8-9.

[37] Bullock, *Fifty Years of Service* 1.

[38] Bullock, *Fifty Years of Service* 2.

[39] Bullock, *Eighty-five Years* 7.

[40] Fancher 72.

[41] Bullock, *Eighty-five Years* 11.

[42] Theodore Morrison, *Chautauqua: A Center for Education, Religion and the Art* (Chicago: University of Chicago Press, 1974) 91.

[43] Morrison 92.

[44] Morrison 94.

[45] Mary Frances Bestor Cram, *Chautauqua Salute: A Memoir of the Bestor Years* (Falconer: Chautauqua Press 1990) 72.

[46] Crocker and Currie 103.

[47] Cram 73.

[48] Morrison 94.

[49] Morrison 94.

[50] Cram 73.

[51] Ida Husted Harper, *The Life and Work of Susan B. Anthony* (New York: Bowen-Merrill) Vol. 2, 727.

[52] Harper 728.

[53] Morrison 92-93.

[54] Irwin 12.

[55] Irwin 11.

[56] Bob Marcotte, "Anthony Steers Suffrage to 'Practical Test,'" *Democrat and Chronicle*, 25 Aug. 2008, 1B.

[57] Irwin 18.

[58] Bullock, *Eighty-five Years* 11-12.

[59] Bullock, *Eighty-five Years* 11.

[60] The General Federation of Women's Clubs official website, 2008.

[61] Cram 101.

[62] Bullock, *Fifty Years of Service* 4.

[63] Cram 13.

[64] Bullock, *Eighty-five Years* 12.

[65] Simpson 86.

[66] Jon Schmitz, personal interview at the Oliver Archives, 18 Aug. 2008.

[67] Bullock, *Eighty-five Years* 13.

[68] Bullock, *Eighty-five Years* 14.

[69] Bullock, *Eighty-five Years* 14-15.

[70] Sophia Smith Collection of Smith College,
http://asteria.fivecolleges.edu/findaids/sophiasmith/mnsss124_bioghist.html

[71] Bullock, *Eighty-five Years* 15-16.

[72] Cram 101.

[73] Bullock, *Eighty-five Years* 16.

[74] Bullock, *Eighty-five Years* 16.

[75] Bullock, *Eighty-five Years* 17.

[76] Bullock, *Eighty-five Years* 17.

[77] Bullock, *Eighty-five Years* 27-28.

[78] Irwin 29.

[79] Irwin 30.

[80] Irwin 31.

[81] Fancher 70.

[82] Irwin 31-33.

[83] Bullock, *Eighty-five Years* 19.

[84] AAUW official website, 2008.

[85] Bullock, *Eighty-five Years* 20-21.

[86] Bullock, *Eighty-Five Years* 22.

[87] Bullock, *Eighty-five Years* 23.

[88] Irwin 35.

[89] Bullock, *Eighty-five Years* 23.

[90] Irwin 37.

[91] Irwin 37.

[92] Irwin 38.

[93] Meredith Rousseau, personal interview, 18 Aug. 2008.

[94] Marjorie Kemper, email correspondence, 27 Jan. 2009.

[95] Marjorie Kemper, email.

[96] Marjorie Kemper, email.

[97] Mary Kunze, email letter, 18 Oct. 2008.

[98] Anita Ferguson, phone interview 20 Jan. 2007.

[99] Ferguson interview.

[100] Lois Vidaver, *The Chautauquan Daily*, 9 Aug. 2006, A3.

[98] Joan Keogh, CWC House Committee Report, 2003.

BIBLIOGRAPHY/WORKS CITED

American Association of University Women. Official website. Oct. 2008. *https://svc.aauw.org/museum/index.cfm*

Bullock, E. Dorothy Dann. *Fifty Years Service of the Club House.* Chautauqua Women's Club, July 27, 1979.

_____. *The History of Eighty-Five Years: 1889-1974. Chautauqua Women's Club, 1974.*

Cram, Mary Frances Bestor. *Chautauqua Salute: A Memoir of the Bestor Years.* Falconer, New York: Chautauqua Press, 1990.

Coda, Roger. photo 25 July 2008.

Crocker, Kathleen and Jane Currie. *Images of America Chautauqua Institution.* Charleston, South Carolina: Arcadia Publishing Company, 2001.

Crowder, Karen. Personal interview at Chautauqua Institution. 17 Aug. 2008.

Fancher, Pauline. Chautauqua: *Its Architecture and People.* Miami: Banyan Books, 1978.

Ferguson, Anita. Personal interview. 20 Jan. 2007.

Fisher, Abigail S. Photographer. photo June 2008.

Flood, T. C., ed. *Chautauqua Assembly Herald.* Vol. 15 advance number. May 1890.

_____. *Chautauqua Assembly Herald.* Vol. 15. 23 July 1890, 8.

_____. *Chautauqua Assembly Herald.* Vol. 15. 26 July 1890, 4.

_____. *Chautauqua Assembly Herald.* Vol. 15. 8 Aug. 1890.

General Federation of Women's Clubs. Official website, 2008.

Gerwig, George William. *Chautauqua: An Appreciation.* East Aurora, New York: Roycrofters, 1924, 21.

Irwin, Alfreda. *Chautauqua Women's Club History 1889-1989.* Chautauqua Women's Club, 1989.

_____. *Three Taps of the Gavel: Pledge to the Future.* Chautauqua Institution, 1987.

Kemper, Marjorie, email correspondence, 27 Jan. 2009.

Keogh, Joan. CWC House Committee Report, 2003.

Kunze, Mary Monsen. E-mail letter/interview. Oct. 2008.

Leone, Paul and Mary Poshka. *Around Chautauqua Lake.* Westfield, New York: Regional Press, 1999.

Marcotte, Bob. *Democrat and Chronicle.* "Anthony Steers Suffrage to 'Practical Test.'" 25 Aug. 2008, 1B.

Morrison, Theodore. *Chautauqua: A Center for Education, Religion and the Arts.* Chicago: University of Chicago Press, 1974.

Navetta, Jean-Marie. "Founding Mothers," *AAUW Outlook.* Spring/Summer 2006, 11-12.

Ross, Alice. "The Mysterious Disappearance of Lard." *Hearth to Hearth* Feb. 2002.

Schmitz, Jon. Personal interview. 18 Aug. 2008.

Simpson, Jeffrey. *Chautauqua an American Utopia.* New York: Harry N. Abrams Inc. 1999.

Sophia Smith Collection, Smith College, http://asteria.fivecolleges.edu/findaids/sophiasmith/mnsss124_bioghist.html

Vidaver, Lois. *Chautauquan Daily.* 9 Aug. 2006, A3.

Women's Christian Temperance Union. Official website, Oct. 2008: http://www.wctu.org/earlyhistory.html

INDEX

About the Author

Janet Northrup was raised in Jamestown and often attended Pops Concerts, church services and musical events at nearby Chautauqua. She worked at the St. Elmo Hotel and the Chautauqua Boys and Girls' Club during college vacations. She taught English at Fairport High School in Fairport, New York for thirty-four years where she served as English Department Lead Teacher. Mrs. Northrup co-authored the District's Style Sheet, vocabulary series, Writing Unit book and (edited/advised) the poetry magazine. She published articles on teaching research techniques in high school in *English Journal*. Her husband and two sons also are English teachers. Janet enjoyed learning about the twenty capable CWC Presidents who contributed in various ways to national women's movements. She explains, "At Chautauqua, history is palpable" and wonders why a book had not been written about the Club's historic influence. She learned how today's Chautauqua women continue to influence Chautauqua and national issues, especially through the Contemporary Issues Forum.

"This history is dedicated to the consecrated leaders and hundreds of loyal and faithful Chautauqua women who, by their gifts of time, talents and money have made possible the...life of the Chautauqua Women's Club." –Dr. E. Dorothy Dann Bullock

Chautauqua Women's Club
P.O. Box R
30 South Lake Dr.
Chautauqua, NY 14722

website: www.chautauquawomensclub.org
email: cwcwomen@gmail.com
phone: 716.357.4961 (during season)